For Babies

Cards shown on page 1

You'll need:
Fabric
Zweigart Art 3882 KLOSTERN, 10 cm (3⅞″) square, left card⋯geranium red, right card⋯off white.
Thread
Anchor 6 strand embroidery floss;
Left card⋯muscat green (0281,0924), caramel (0888,0906,0885) and cardinal (020) small amount of each.
Right card⋯muscat green (0281, 0279), caramel (0888), cyclamen (087,086), lilac (0105) and violet (098) small amount of each.
Fitting
Drawing paper 22 cm × 15 cm (8⅝″ × 5⅞″), copper green for left card, muscat green for right.

Finished size
15 cm × 11 cm (5⅞″ × 4⅜″).
Directions
Match centers of fabric and pattern; embroider as shown.

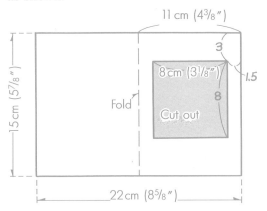

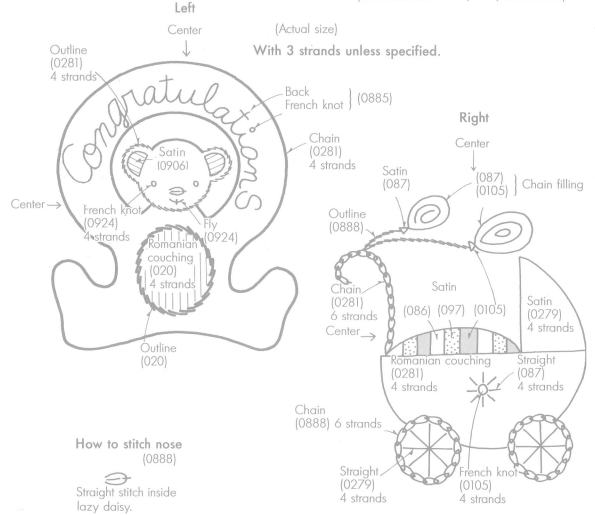

Left
Center
(Actual size)
With 3 strands unless specified.

Outline (0281) 4 strands
Back French knot } (0885)
Satin (0906)
Chain (0281) 4 strands
French knot (0924) 4 strands
Fly (0924)
Romanian couching (020) 4 strands
Center →
Center
Outline (020)

Right
Center
Satin (087)
(087) (0105) } Chain filling
Outline (0888)
Chain (0281) 6 strands
Center →
Satin (086) (097) (0105)
Satin (0279) 4 strands
Romanian couching (0281) 4 strands
Straight (087) 4 strands
Chain (0888) 6 strands
Straight (0279) 4 strands
French knot (0105) 4 strands

How to stitch nose (0888)

Straight stitch inside lazy daisy.

Bags (E, F) shown on page 21

You'll need:

Fabric

E···cotton cloth, sky blue printed fabric } 46 cm × 28 cm each ($18^1/_8$″ × $11^1/_{16}$″).

F···cotton cloth, soft pink printed fabric } 46 cm × 28 cm each ($18^1/_8$″ × $11^1/_{16}$″).

Thread

DMC 6 strand embroidery floss;

E···indigo (334) 1 skein, indigo (312, 311), old rose (3350), parma violet (208), emerald green (911), old gold (680), lemon yellow (307), tangerine yellow (741) and umber (434) small amount of each.

F···magenta rose (963) 1 skein, magenta rose (962), pistachio green (890), parakeet green (905) and umber (434) small amount of each.

Fitting

Adhesive backing 46 cm × 15 cm ($18^1/_8$″ × $5^7/_8$″) (for each). Ribbon, 1 cm ($3/_8$″) width, 65 cm ($25^5/_8$″) length, sky blue for E, soft pink for F.

Finished size

25 cm in depth ($9^7/_8$″).

Directions.

Cut fabric and assemble as shown.

Assembly

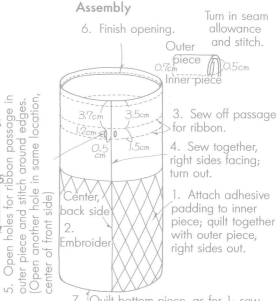

6. Finish opening.

Turn in seam allowance and stitch.

3. Sew off passage for ribbon.

4. Sew together, right sides facing; turn out.

1. Attach adhesive padding to inner piece; quilt together with outer piece, right sides out.

2. Embroider

7. Quilt bottom piece, as for 1; sew onto side piece, right sides facing.

8. Pass ribbon through opening.

E

Seam allowance 1.2 (0.5 for inner piece)

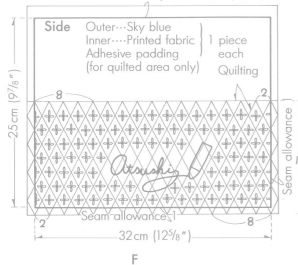

Side — Outer···Sky blue / Inner····Printed fabric / Adhesive padding (for quilted area only) } 1 piece each — Quilting

25 cm ($9^7/_8$″)

8 — 2

Seam allowance 1

Seam allowance 1

2 — 8

32 cm ($12^5/_8$″)

15

Open holes for ribbon passage in outer piece and stitch around edges. (Open another hole in same location, center of front side)

F

Seam allowance 1.2 (0.5 for inner piece)

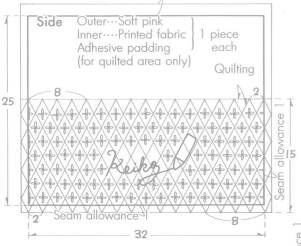

Side — Outer····Soft pink / Inner····Printed fabric / Adhesive padding (for quilted area only) } 1 piece each — Quilting

25

8 — 2

Seam allowance 1

2 — 8

32

15

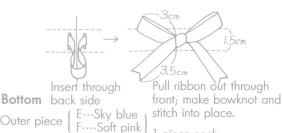

Insert through back side

Pull ribbon out through front; make bowknot and stitch into place.

Bottom

Outer piece { E···Sky blue / F····Soft pink / Inner piece····Printed fabric / Adhesive padding } 1 piece each

Seam allowance 1

Quilting

10

Patterns same as for Lunch Pouches, shown on p. 23.

Bottle Cover
shown on page 4

You'll need:

Fabric
Zweigart Art 1008 SOLTA, White, 34 cm × 27 cm (13³/₈″ × 10⁵/₈″). White flannel, 34 cm × 23 cm (13³/₈″ × 9¹/₁₆″).

Thread
Anchor 6 strand embroidery floss; carnation (026), kingfisher (0159), lido blue (0433), canary yellow (0289, 0291) and grass green (0242) small amount of each.

Fitting
White twisted string, 0.3 cm (¹/₈″) diameter, 55 cm (21⁵/₈″) length. White lace, 3.5 cm (1³/₈″) width, 43 cm (16⁷/₈″) length.

Finished size
Refter to chart.

Directions
Embroider onto side piece, according to pattern; assemble as shown.

Assembly

Measurements inside parenthesis indicate seam allowance; add 1 cm unless otherwise noted.

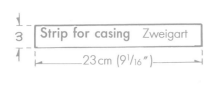

Strip for casing   Zweigart

23 cm (9¹/₁₆″)

3

Side

(6 cm for lining piece) Front piece···Zweigart } 1 piece each
Lining piece···Flannel

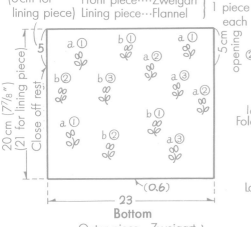

20 cm (7⁷/₈″) (21 for lining piece)

Close off rest

5 cm opening

23

(0.6)

Bottom

Outer piece···Zweigart } 1 piece each
Lining piece···Flannel

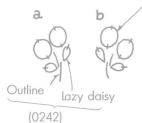

(0.6)

7

(Actual size)
Use 4 strands of floss

a   b

Irregular lazy daisy
(see directions for Bib)

Outline   Lazy daisy

(0242)

Flower colors

	Left	Right
1.	(026)	(026)
2.	(0433)	(0159)
3.	(0291)	(0289)

① Strip for casing (Front)

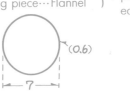

1 cm

Lace

Fold back seam allowance; machine stitch onto side piece, catching in ruffled lace.

② a Sew together inner piece and strip for casing.

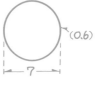

Inner piece

b Machine stitch into place.

1 cm
Fold   Casing
1 cm
2 cm
c

Lace   Side

Fold back seam allowance of both sides and machine stitch edtes.

③ Assemble pieces with right sides facing for outer and inner pieces respectively; sew up side opening and attach bottom.

④ Straighten shape and finish edges of opening; make casing.

a
b Machine stitch into place.

Fold back seam allowance and machine stitch.

When finished:

Pass through twisted string.

22 cm
2 cm
2.5 cm
7 cm
7 cm

Cap shown on page 5

You'll need:
Purchesed baby cap.
Thread
Anchor 6 strand embroidery floss;
carnation (025, 024, 026), canary yellow (0291), kingfisher (0159), parrot green (0254) and white small amount of each.
Directions
Copy patterns symmetrically onto left and right side pieces; embroider.

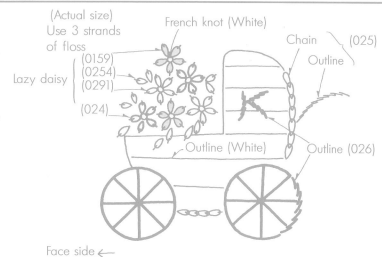

(Actual size)
Use 3 strands of floss
French knot (White)
Chain (025)
Outline
Lazy daisy (0159) (0254) (0291)
(024)
Outline (White)
Outline (026)
Face side ←

Bib shown on page 5

You'll need:
Purchased bib.
Thread
Anchor 6 strand embroidery floss;
carnation (026, 024), parrot green (8254) and white small amount of each.
Directions
Position and copy pattern onto bib, according to photograph; embroider.

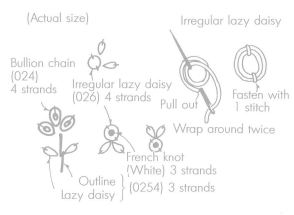

(Actual size)
Irregular lazy daisy
Bullion chain (024) 4 strands
Irregular lazy daisy (026) 4 strands
Pull out
Fasten with 1 stitch
Wrap around twice
French knot (White) 3 strands
Outline Lazy daisy } (0254) 3 strands

Mittens shown on page 5

You'll need:
Purchased baby mittens.
Thread
Anchor 6 strand embroidery floss;
canary yellow (0291, 0289), carnation (025), kingfisher (0159) and grass green (0242) small amount of each.
Directions
Copy pattern symmetrically onto left and right pieces; embroider.

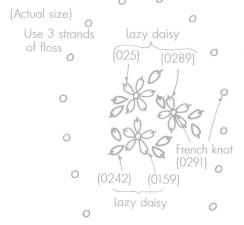

(Actual size)
Use 3 strands of floss
Lazy daisy
(025) (0289)
French knot (0291)
(0242) (0159)
Lazy daisy

Sox shown on page 5

You'll need:
Purchased (store bought) baby sox.
Thread
Anchor 6 strand embroidery floss;
canary yellow (0291) and grass green (0242) small amount of each.
Directions
Make five embroideries each, according to pattern, around folded area.

(Actual size)
Bullion chain (0291) 3 strands
Lazy daisy } (0242)
Straight } 3 strands

Towel Cats and Towel Trains★Instructions on pages 11 and 66.

Pillow Case and Blanket Guard★Instructions on page 84.

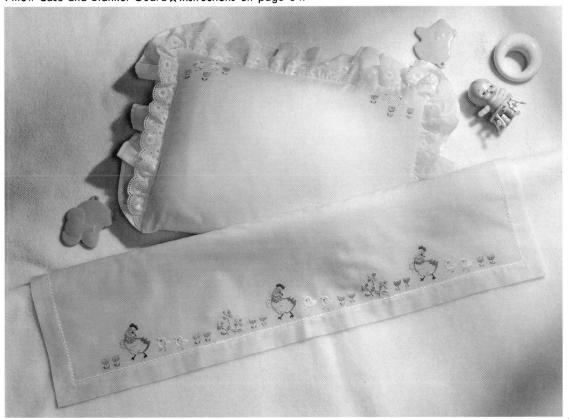

Towel   shown on page 8

You'll need:
Cream-colored towel, 35 cm (13¾") square.
Thread
Anchor 6 strand embroidery floss;

apricot (4146), tangerine (0313), carnation (024, 023, 025, 026), peacock blue (0167), turquoise (0928), laurel green (0208), gray (0401) and white small amount of each.

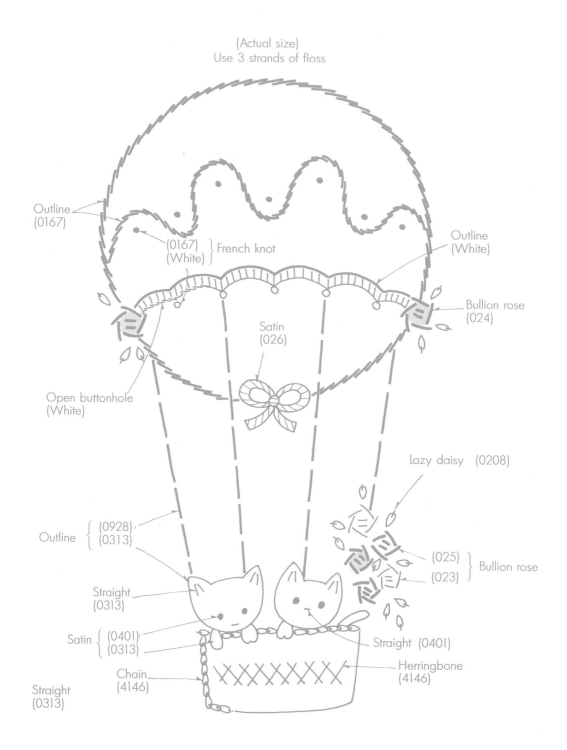

(Actual size)
Use 3 strands of floss

Outline (0167)

(0167) (White) } French knot

Outline (White)

Bullion rose (024)

Satin (026)

Open buttonhole (White)

Lazy daisy (0208)

Outline { (0928) (0313)

(025) (023) } Bullion rose

Straight (0313)

Satin { (0401) (0313)

Straight (0401)

Chain (4146)

Herringbone (4146)

Straight (0313)

Towel Cats

You'll need:

Fabric

White cotton terrycloth, 20 cm (7⅞″) square for 1 towel cat. Broadcloth 13 cm × 5 cm (5⅛″ × 2″), peony rose for left cat, sky blue for right.

Thread

DMC 6 strand embroidery floss;

Left cat···geranium pink (894), soft pink (818), chocolate (632), chestnut (407, 950) and almond green (504) small amount of each.

Right cat···chocolate (632), chestnut (407, 950), cornflower blue (794), foget-me-not blue (828), geranium pink (894) and almond green (504) small amount of each.

Fitting

Ribbon 0.7 cm (¼″) in width, 13 cm (5⅛″) length, soft pink for left, sky blue for right.

Finished size

Refer to chart.

Directions

Sew together front and back pieces for head and body, both with right sides facing; leave opening for stuffing. Turn right-side-out and stuff. Attach head onto body, and arrange face to desired expression. Sew on embroidery fabric for clothing, and attach ribbon onto head.

Patterns (Actual size)

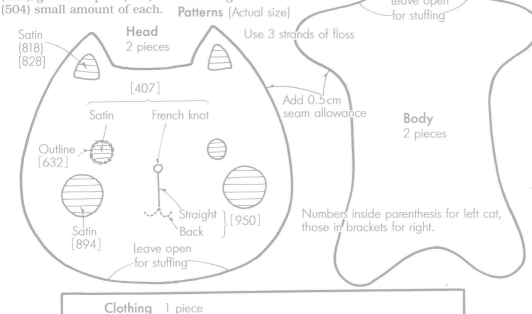

Satin (818) [828]

Head
2 pieces

Use 3 strands of floss

leave open for stuffing

[407]

Satin   French knot

Outline [632]

Add 0.5 cm seam allowance

Body
2 pieces

Straight
Back } [950]

Satin [894]

Leave open for stuffing

Numbers inside parenthesis for left cat, those in brackets for right.

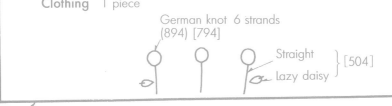

Clothing   1 piece

German knot 6 strands
(894) [794]

Straight
Lazy daisy } [504]

Add 1 cm margin all around   **When finished:**

Attach ribbon

13 cm
(5⅛″)

Stitch closed

Miniature Frames shown on pages 12–13

You'll need:
Fabric
Zweigart Art 3609 BELFAST, 15 cm × 13 cm (5⅞″ × 5⅛″), off-white for left, faded pink for right.
Thread
Anchor 6 strand embroidery floss;
Left frame···kingfisher (0160), cobalt blue (0131, 0134), muscat green (0278), carnation (023, 026), cinnamon (0367), gorse yellow (0303) and white small amount of each.

Right frame···raspberry (068, 066), cyclamen (087), jade (0185), moss green (0266), cornflower (0145), lichen green (0853) and amber gold (0305) small amount of each.
Fitting
Frames, inner size 8.5 cm × 7 cm (3⅜″ × 2¾″).
Finished size
Same as frame size.
Directions
Copy pattern and embroider; frame when completed.

Left

(Actual size)

Outline stitch unless otherwise noted
Use 3 strands of floss unless otherwise noted

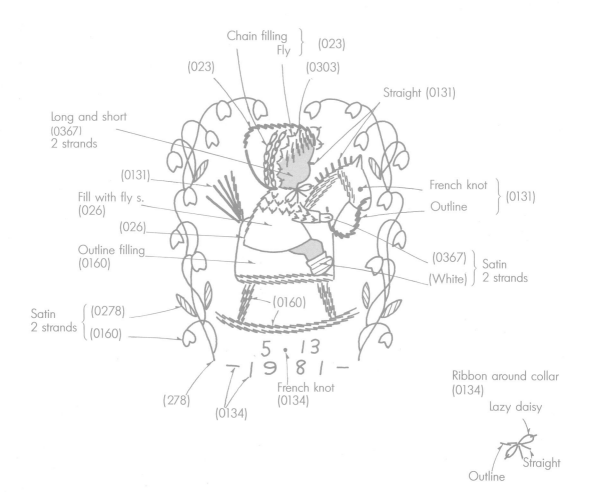

To frame, fold back fabric edges and finish as shown.

(Back side)

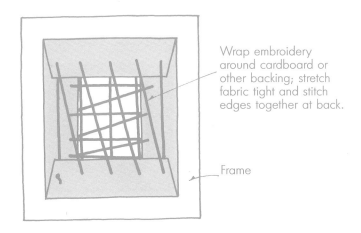

Wrap embroidery around cardboard or other backing; stretch fabric tight and stitch edges together at back.

Frame

Right

(Actual size)

Use 3 strands of floss unless otherwise noted.

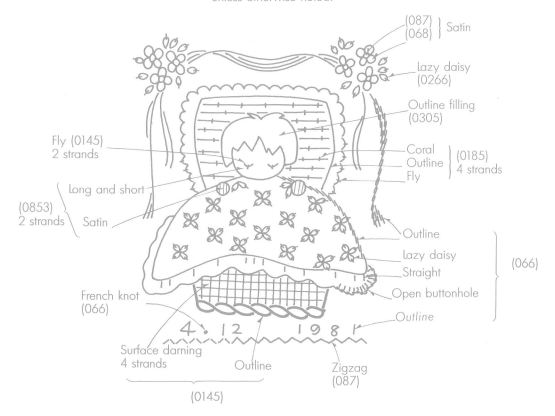

(087)
(068) } Satin

Lazy daisy (0266)

Outline filling (0305)

Fly (0145) 2 strands

Coral
Outline } (0185)
Fly } 4 strands

Long and short

(0853) 2 strands

Satin

Outline

Lazy daisy

Straight (066)

Open buttonhole

French knot (066)

Outline

Surface darning 4 strands

Outline

Zigzag (087)

(0145)

4 . 12   198

SNOOPY

Cards★Instructions on page 71.

For Kindergarteners

16

Album★Instructions on page 18.

Album shown on page 17

You'll need:

Fabric
Off-white cotton satin, 39 cm × 91 cm (15³/₈" × 35⁷/₈")

Thread
Anchor 6 strand embroidery floss; gorse yellow (0304, 0301), tangerine (0311), apricot (0868, 4146), carnation (026, 027, 029, 024, 025), violet (095), lilac (0104), jade (0185), laurel green (0208), moss green (0265), canary yellow (0290), gray (0401) and white small amount of each.

Finished size
38 cm × 29 cm (15" × 11³/₈").

Directions
Embroider according to pattern. Have completed embroidery fitted onto album.

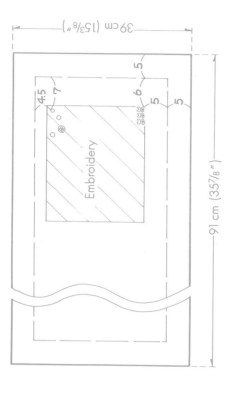

Embroidery

39 cm (15³/₈")

91 cm (35⁷/₈")

4.5 7 5 5 6 5 5

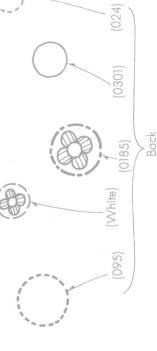

Back

(024)

(0301)

(0185)

(White)

(095)

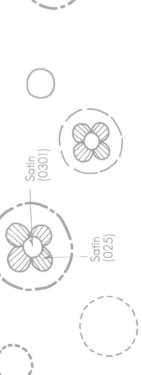

Satin (0301)

Satin (025)

(Actual size)

Use 3 strands of floss unless otherwise noted

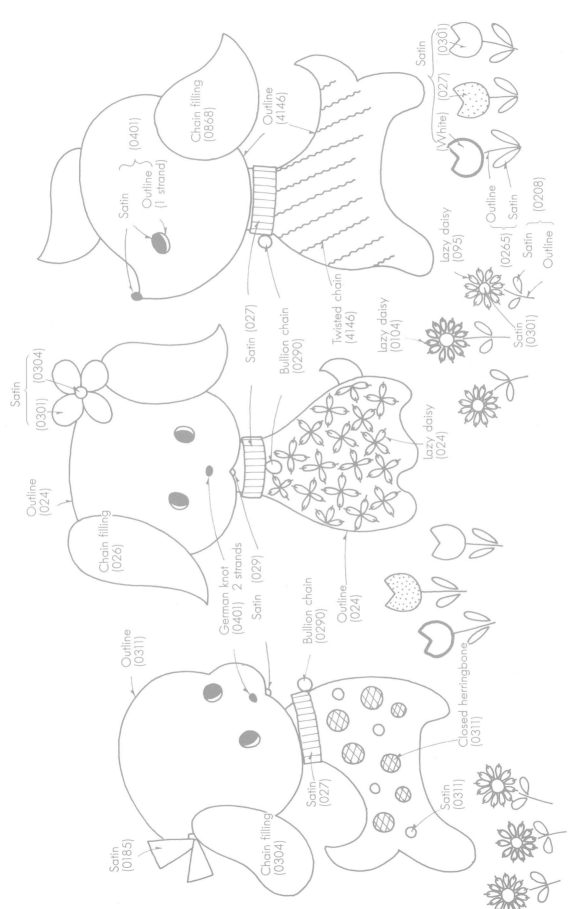

Satin (0401)

Satin } Outline (1 strand)

Chain filling (0868)

Outline (4146)

Satin (027)

Bullion chain (0290)

Twisted chain (4146)

Lazy daisy (0104)

Lazy daisy (095)

Satin (0301)

White (027) (0301)

Outline } Satin (0265)

Satin } (0208) Outline

Satin (0301)

Satin (0301) (0304)

Outline (024)

Chain filling (026)

German knot (0401) 2 strands

Satin (029)

Bullion chain (0290)

Outline (024)

Lazy daisy (024)

Outline (0311)

Satin (0185)

Chain filling (0304)

Satin (027)

Satin (0311)

Closed herringbone (0311)

19

Pochette(A), Bag(B), Lunch Pouches(C, D) and Bags(E, F)

structions on pages 72(A), 74(B), 22(C, D) and 3(E, F).

E

F

D

Lunch Pouches (C, D) shown on pages 20-21

You'll need:

Fabric

C···pink cotton cloth, 32 cm (12⅝″) square. Printed inner fabric, 30 cm × 22 cm (11¾″ × 8⅝″).

D···sky blue cotton cloth, 32 cm (12⅝″) square.

Thread

DMC 6 strand embroidery floss;

C···magenta rose (963, 962), pistachio green (890), parakeet green (905) and umber (434) small amount of each.

D···indigo (334, 312, 311), old rose (3350), parma violet (208), emerald green (911), old gold (680), lemon yellow (307) and tangerine yellow (741) small amount of each.

Fitting (for each)

Adhesive backing 32 cm × 10 cm (12⅝″ × 3⅞″). Bias tape 1.2 cm (½″) in width, 40 cm (15¾″) length, pink for C, blue for D.

Finished size

Refer to chart.

Directions

Cut fabric and assemble as shown.

Assembly

① Fold outer piece in half, right side in; sew both edges.

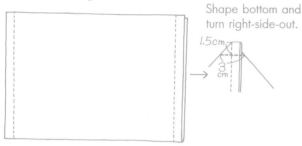

Shape bottom and turn right-side-out.

1.5cm

3 cm

② Sew inner piece in same manner.

Front and back

Outer piece
1 piece

      C···Pink
      D···Sky blue

Inner piece
1 piece

      Printed fabric

Seam allowance 1

28 cm (11″)

20cm (7⅞″)

③ Make flap

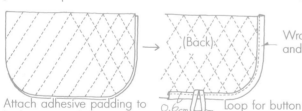

Attach adhesive padding to both outer and inner pieces; quilt with right sides out.

(Back)

Wrap bias tape around edges and machine stitch.

0.6cm — Loop for button

7cm — 0.6cm

Fold bias tape in half; machine stitch edge.

④ Embroider

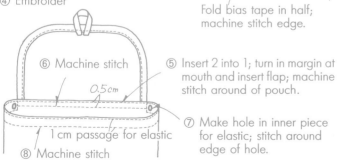

⑥ Machine stitch

0.5cm

1 cm passage for elastic

⑧ Machine stitch

⑤ Insert 2 into 1; turn in margin at mouth and insert flap; machine stitch around of pouch.

⑦ Make hole in inner piece for elastic; stitch around edge of hole.

16cm (6¼″)

9cm (3½″)

12.5cm (4⅞″)

8cm

⑩ Attach button

20cm

3cm

⑨ Pass through elastic and stitch sides closed.

Flap (Actual size)

C Outer and inner pieces···Pink, 1 piece each.
Adhesive padding 2 pieces.

Use 3 strands of floss

(Outer 905, Inner 890)

Double lazy daisy
(Outer 962, Inner 963)

Seam allowance

French knot
(962)

Outline
(434)

Quilting

Chain   Satin
(962)

Lazy daisy
(963)

D Outer, inner pieces···Sky blue, 1 piece each.
Adhesive padding 2 pieces.

Chain
(a.741, b.307, c.680, d.911, e.312, f.208, g.3350)

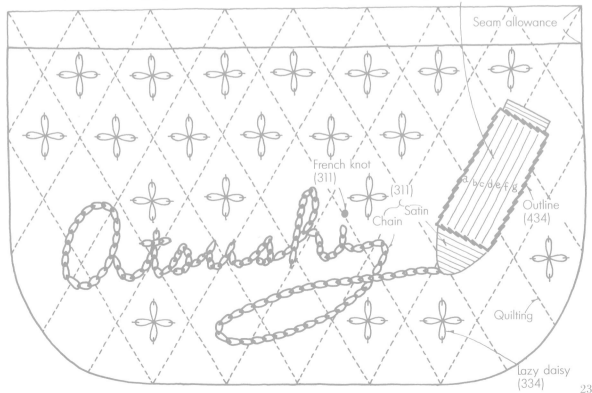

Seam allowance

French knot
(311)

(311)

Satin

Chain

a/b/c/d/e/f/g

Outline
(434)

Quilting

Lazy daisy
(334)

23

Happy Birthday

Cards★Instructions on page 26.

Bookcover and Bookmarks★Instructions on pages 76 and 27.

Cards   shown on page 24

You'll need:
Fabric
Zweigart Art 3882 KLOSTERN, 10cm (3⅞″)
square, royal blue for left, umber for right.
Thread
Anchor 6 strand embroidery floss;
Left card···moss green (0268, 0267, 0266),
muscat green (0278), caramel (0906) and pea-
cock blue (0168) small amount of each.
Right···cyclamen (087, 088), lilac (0107), vio-
let (098), lichen green (0853) and moss green
(0267) small amount of each.

Fitting
Drawing paper 22cm × 15cm (8⅝″ × 5⅞″),
brilliant green for left, tangerine yellow for
right.
Finished size
15cm × 11cm (5⅞″ × 4⅜″).
Directions
See directions for Card on page 2.

Pull out approx. 1cm of thread on both
sides; cut to make fringes.

Left

1cm

Use 4 strands of floss unless
otherwise noted

(Actual size)   Outline
6 strands

(0266)
(0267)
(0268)

Outline
(0906)

←Center

Chain
(0168)

Right

Chain
(0278)

Outline filling
(0906)

↑
Center

Back

(0267)   (087)
3 strands   2 strands

Happy Birthday

Center→

Chain
(0853)
4 strands

↑
Center

Straight st. with 3 strands of extra fine
reddish purple yarn.

3cm

Wrap around 3 strands
2½ times; tie at center
and attach.

⊙ (0107)
○ (098)   ⎫ French knot
● (088)   ⎬ 6 strands
⊗ (087)   ⎭

Bookmarks shown on page 25

You'll need:
Fabric
Broadcloth···Top: pink flower patterned 21 cm × 11 cm (8¼″ × 4⅜″), bits of white. Bottom: blue flower patterned 19 cm × 11 cm (7½″ × 4⅜″), bits of white.

Thread
DMC 6 strand embroidery floss;
Top···saffron (726, 727), geranium pink (894), soft pink (818), mahogany (402), pistachio green (320), parma violet (208) and black small amount of each.
Bottom···geranium pink (894), pistachio green (320), plum (554), beige brown (842), beaver gray (648) and mahogany (400) small amount of each.

Fitting
Adhesive backing, 21 cm square (8¼″) for top, 19 cm square (7½″) for bottom; grosgrain ribbon 0.6 cm (¼″) in width, 16 cm (6¼″) in length, canary yellow for top, indigo for bottom.

Directions
Copy pattern onto white broadcloth and embroider; Attach adhesive padding to back and cut, leaving margin for sewing. For flower pattern broadcloth, attach adhesive padding and cut for top; for bottom, cut second piece symmetrically. Cut opening in front pieces only and place over white embroidered broadcloth; stitch in place. Match front and back pieces and zig-zag machine stitch around edges, folding in grosgrain ribbon where indicated.

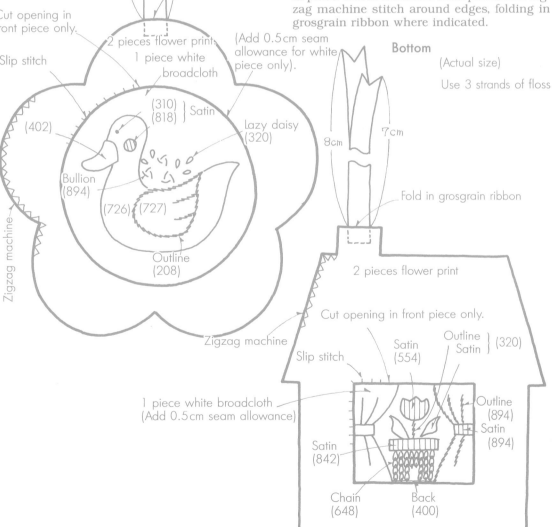

Top
(Actual size)
Use 3 strands of floss and outline filling stitch unless otherwise noted.

Fold in grosgrain ribbon.

8cm 7cm

Cut opening in front piece only.

Slip stitch

2 pieces flower print,
1 piece white broadcloth

(Add 0.5 cm seam allowance for white piece only).

(402)

(310)
(818) } Satin

Lazy daisy (320)

Bullion (894)

(726) (727)

Zigzag machine

Outline (208)

Zigzag machine

Bottom
(Actual size)
Use 3 strands of floss

8cm 7cm

Fold in grosgrain ribbon

2 pieces flower print

Cut opening in front piece only.

Slip stitch

Satin (554)

Outline
Satin } (320)

1 piece white broadcloth
(Add 0.5 cm seam allowance)

Outline (894)

Satin (894)

Satin (842)

Chain (648)

Back (400)

Instructions on pages 83(A, B), 78(C, D) and 30(E, F).

B

D

E

F

29

Tissue Paper Case (E) shown on page 29

You'll need:

Fabric

Light silk, tangerine yellow, 25 cm × 18 cm ($9\frac{7}{8}'' \times 7\frac{1}{16}''$). Rayon lining fabric, 18 cm × 14 cm ($7\frac{1}{16}'' \times 5\frac{1}{2}''$).

Thread

Anchor 6 strand embroidery floss; carnation (029, 028, 027, 026, 024) and winter green (0876, 0877, 0878) small amount of each.

Fitting

White satin ribbon 0.9 cm in width, 72 cm ($28\frac{3}{8}''$) length. White tatting lace 1.3 cm ($\frac{1}{2}''$) in width, 100 cm ($39\frac{3}{8}''$) length. Purchased flower appliqués of pink and blue, 1 each.

Finished size

12.5 cm × 9 cm ($4\frac{7}{8}'' \times 3\frac{1}{2}''$).

Measurements inside parenthesis indicate seam allowance.

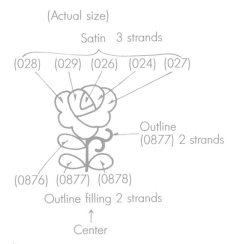

(Actual size)

Satin 3 strands

(028) (029) (026) (024) (027)

Outline (0877) 2 strands

(0876) (0877) (0878)

Outline filling 2 strands

↑ Center

Directions

Copy pattern onto outer fabric, placing design symmetrically as shown; embroider and assemble as below.

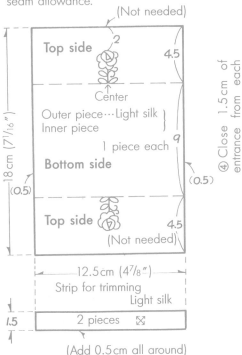

Assembly

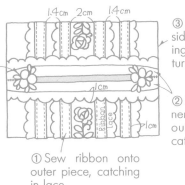

③ Join top and bottom sides, right sides facing; sew together and turn out.

② Match outer and inner pieces, right sides out; trim entrance, catching in lace.

① Sew ribbon onto outer piece, catching in lace.

 # Eyeglass Case (F) shown on page 29

You'll need:

Fabric

Light silk, tangerine yellow, 18 cm × 24 cm ($7\frac{1}{16}'' \times 9\frac{1}{2}''$). Rayon lining fabric, 18 cm × 25 cm ($7\frac{1}{16}'' \times 9\frac{7}{8}''$).

Thread

Anchor 6 strand embroidery floss; carnation (029, 028, 027, 026, 024), winter green (0878, 0877, 0876) and peacock blue (169, 0167) small amount of each.

Fitting

White satin ribbon, 0.9 cm ($\frac{3}{8}''$) in width, 90 cm ($35\frac{3}{8}''$) length. White tatting lace, 1.3 cm ($\frac{1}{2}''$) in width, 105 cm ($41\frac{3}{8}''$) length. 1 pink purchased flower appliqués. 1 pair small snap buttons.

Finished size

18.5 cm × 8 cm ($7\frac{1}{4}'' \times 3\frac{1}{8}''$).

Directions

Copy pattern onto flap and front side of outer piece; embroider and assemble as shown.

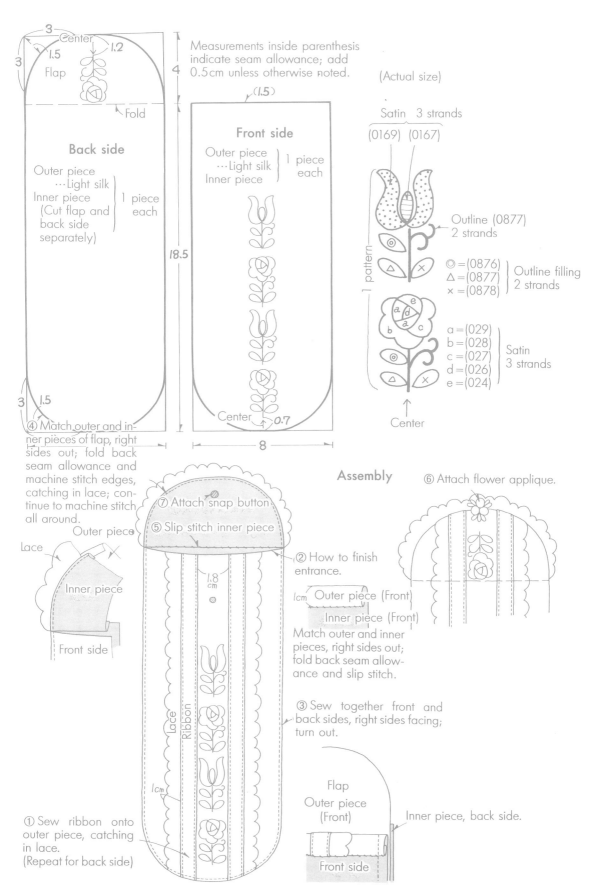

F

E

Sachets shown on page 32

A

You'll need:

Fabric
White silk satin, 14 cm × 11 cm (5¹/₂″ × 4³/₈″).
Thread
Anchor 6 strand embroidery floss;
moss green (0266), sea blue (0978), kingfisher
(0158, 0160), cobalt blue (0130) and violet (095)
small amount of each.
Fitting
Small round beads, light blue, blue velvet
ribbon, 22 cm (8⁵/₈″) in length.
Finished size
9.5 cm (3³/₄″) in depth.
Directions
Cut out fabric; copy pattern onto front side; embroider and sew on beads. Sew on beads as
desired on back side. Sew front and back pieces
together, right sides facing, leaving mouth
open; turn out. Make fringes by pulling out
horizontal stitches from 0.5 cm (¹/₄″) of sewing
margin at mouth. Tie ribbon to finish.

Use 2 strands of floss unless otherwise noted.
Front piece } 1 piece each
Back piece }

Satin fabric   Add 0.5 cm all around for seam
allowance.

(Actual size)
Front piece }
Back piece }
1 piece each
Satin fabric

Use 2 strands of floss unless
otherwise noted.
Add 0.5 cm all around for seam
allowance.

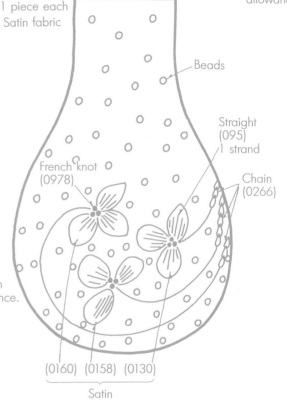

Beads

Straight
(095)
1 strand

Chain
(0266)

French knot
(0978)

(0160) (0158) (0130)

Satin

String guide
Straight
(073) 6 strands

Outline

Satin   (0214)

French knot
(White)

Satin
(095)

(097)
(040) } Satin

(026)
Satin   (0885)

B

You'll need:

Fabric
Soft pink silk satin, 18 cm × 13 cm
(7¹/₈″ × 5¹/₈″).
Thread
Anchor 6 strand embroidery floss;
carnation (026), old rose ((073), cardinal
(040), violet (097, 095), forest green
(0214), caramel (0885) and white small
amount of each.
Fitting
Soft pink lace, 1.5 cm (⁵/₈″) in width,
50 cm (19⁵/₈″) length Soft pink tape,
0.8 cm (³/₈″) width, 11 cm (4³/₈″) length
crochet hook, Milward 14.
Finished size
Refer to chart.
Directions
Cut out fabric; copy pattern onto front
side and embroider; assemble as shown.

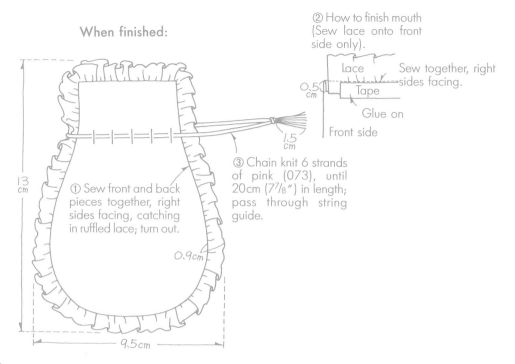

When finished:

② How to finish mouth (Sew lace onto front side only).

Lace — Sew together, right sides facing.

0.5 cm — Tape

Glue on

Front side

① Sew front and back pieces together, right sides facing, catching in ruffled lace; turn out.

③ Chain knit 6 strands of pink (073), until 20cm (7⁷/₈″) in length; pass through string guide.

13 cm

1.5 cm

0.9 cm

9.5 cm

![decorative icon] **Pin Cushions (C)** shown on page 32

You'll need:
Fabric
Silk satin, off-white and pink, 14cm (5¹/₂″) square each.
Thread
Anchor 6 strand embroidery floss; cobalt blue (0130), kingfisher (0158), amber gold (0305), buttercup (0292), lilac (0104), carnation (025), old rose (073), forest green (0214) and white small amount of each.

Use 3 strands of floss and bullion rose stitch unless otherwise noted.

Fitting
Bits of cotton.
Finished size
12cm square (4³/₄″).
Directions
Copy pattern onto center of front piece; embroider. Sew pieces together as shown and stuff with filling. Close off opening and attach tassel to corner.

When finished:

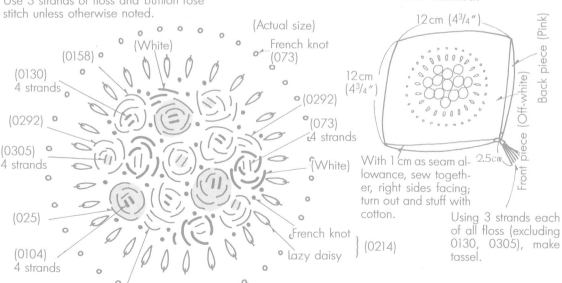

(Actual size)

(White)

French knot (073)

(0158)

(0130) 4 strands

(0292)

(0292)

(073) 4 strands

(0305) 4 strands

(White)

(025)

French knot

(0104) 4 strands

lazy daisy

(0292)

} (0214)

12 cm (4³/₄″)

12 cm (4³/₄″)

Back piece (Pink)

Front piece (Off-white)

2.5cm

With 1cm as seam allowance, sew together, right sides facing; turn out and stuff with cotton.

Using 3 strands each of all floss (excluding 0130, 0305), make tassel.

35

Miniature Frames★Instructions on pages 38(Left), 39(Top) and 81(Right).

Miniature Frames shown on page 37

Left Frame
You'll need:
Fabric
Zweigart Art 3711 ARIOSA, white, 13 cm (5¹⁄₈″) square. Pink cotton cloth, 20 cm (7⁷⁄₈″) square.
Thread
Anchor 6 strand embroidery floss; cyclamen (085), carnation (026), terra-cotta (0336), apple green (0203), jade (0188), parma violet (0108), cobalt blue (0130) and canary yellow (0289) small amount of each.

Fitting
Frame, 14 cm (5¹⁄₂″) square in inner size. White lace, 1.2 cm (¹⁄₂″) in width, 40 cm (15³⁄₄″) length.
Finished size
Same as frame size.
Directions
Match centers of fabric and pattern; copy pattern and embroider. Assemble as shown.

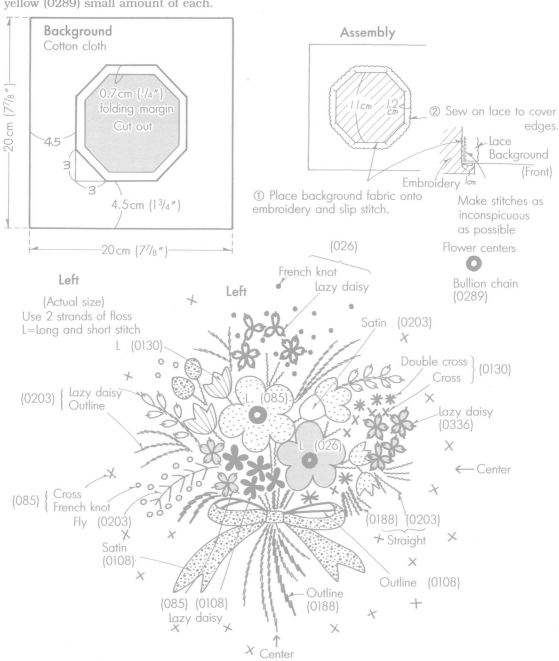

Background Cotton cloth

0.7 cm (¹⁄₄″) folding margin Cut out

20 cm (7⁷⁄₈″)

4.5

3

3

4.5 cm (1³⁄₄″)

20 cm (7⁷⁄₈″)

Assembly

11 cm

1.2 cm

② Sew on lace to cover edges.

Lace
Background (Front)
Embroidery 1 cm

① Place background fabric onto embroidery and slip stitch.

Make stitches as inconspicuous as possible

Flower centers

Bullion chain (0289)

Left

(Actual size)
Use 2 strands of floss
L=Long and short stitch

Left

(026) French knot
Lazy daisy

Satin (0203)

Double cross (0130)
Cross

L (0130)

(0203) { Lazy daisy / Outline

L. (085)

Lazy daisy (0336)

L (026)

← Center

(085) { Cross / French knot
Fly (0203)

(0188) (0203)
Straight

Satin (0108)

Outline (0188)

Outline (0108)

(085) (0108)
Lazy daisy

Center

Top Frame
You'll need:
Fabric
Zweigart Art 3711 ARIOSA, white, 12 cm (4³/₄″) square. Blue cotton cloth, 20 cm (7⁷/₈″) square.
Thread
Anchor 6 strand embroidery floss;
apple green (0203), jade (0185, 0188), geranium (09), flesh pink (0883), terra-cotta (0336), cobalt blue (0130) and parma violet (0108) small amount of each.

Fitting
Frame, 14 cm (5¹/₂″) square in inner.
Finished size
Same as frame size.
Directions
Match centers of fabric and pattern; copy pattern and embroider.

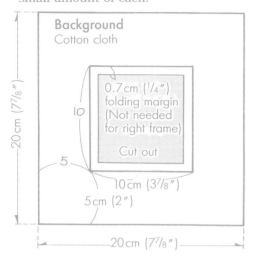

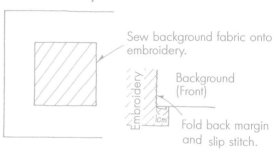

Assembly

Sew background fabric onto embroidery.

Background (Front)

Embroidery

Fold back margin and slip stitch.

(Actual size)

Use 2 strands of floss
Chain filling stitch unless otherwise noted.

Back (0130)

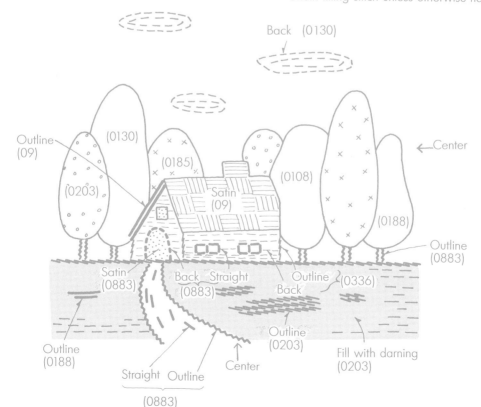

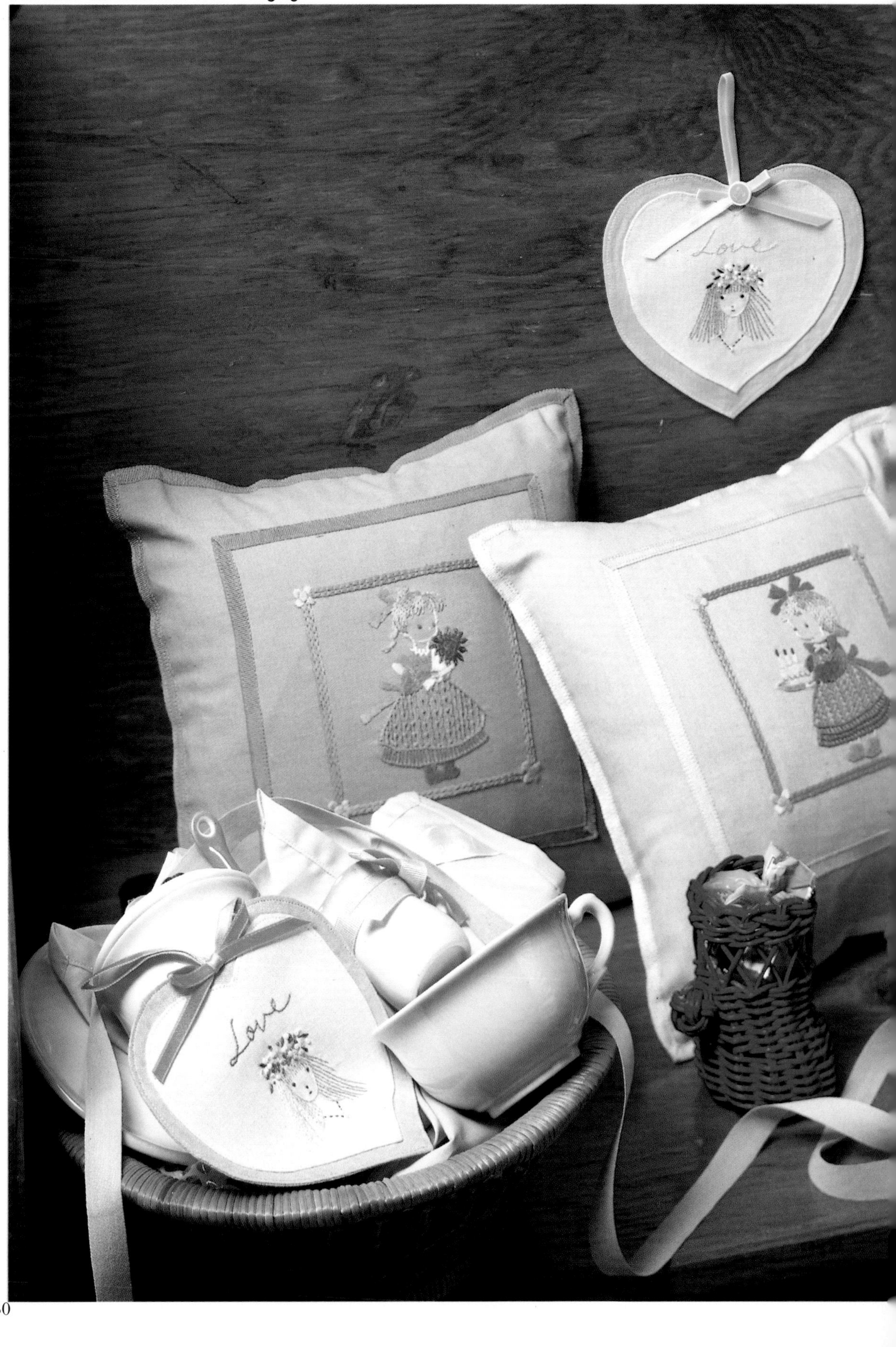
Love
Love

Instructions on pages 42(Miniature Cushions) and 93(Wall Hangings).

Miniature Cushions shown on pages 40-41

You'll need:

Fabric

Cotton cloth, 64 cm × 30 cm (25¼″ × 11¾″), cerise for left cushion, medium cerise for center cushion, light cerise for right cushion.

Thread

Anchor 6 strand embroidery floss;

Left

peacock blue (0167) 0.5 skein, amber gold (0306), canary yellow (0289), emerald (0227), mist green (0861), carnation (026), cobalt blue (0131), rose pink (059) and white small amount of each.

Center

carnation (026) 0.5 skein, cardinal (040), old rose (075), cobalt blue (0131), amber gold (0306), mist green (086), canary yellow (0289), scarlet (046), peacock blue (0167) and white small amount of each.

Right

cardinal (040) 0.5 skein, peacock blue (0167), cobalt blue (0131), amber gold (0306), mist green (0861), scarlet (046), canary yellow (0289) and white small amount of each.

Fitting

Zipper, 24 cm (9½″), grosgrain ribbon 0.7 cm (¼″) in width, 190 cm (74¾″) length.

Finished size

28 cm square (11″).

Directions

1. Copy pattern onto center of front piece and embroider.
2. Sew inner ribbon onto front piece.
3. Attach zipper onto back piece.
4. Match front and back pieces, right sides out; fold in margin and place ribbon around edges; sew together.
5. Stuff with filled inner bag.

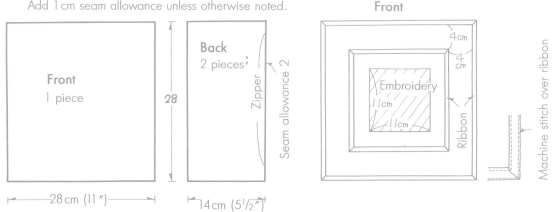

Left (Actual size)

Satin (0289) 2 strands   Use 4 strands of floss unless otherwise noted.

Chain   (0167)

Long and short

Satin (0131) 2 strands

Straight (0306)

(White) { Fly
          Satin
          2 strands

Outline filling
(0167) 3 strands

Satin (0167)
2 strands

Long and short
(026)
3 strands

(0167) { Coral
         Outline

Open buttonhole
(026)

Outline
(0306)

Outline
3 strands
Straight   (0861)
2 strands

French knot
(059) 6 strands

Lazy daisy
(0227) 3 strands

Long and short
(White)

Outline
(0861)   3 strands

Satin (0131)
2 strands

Add 1 cm seam allowance unless otherwise noted.

Front
1 piece

28

28 cm (11″)

Back
2 pieces

Zipper

Seam allowance 2

14 cm (5½″)

Front

4 cm

4 cm

Embroidery

1 cm

1 cm

Ribbon

Machine stitch over ribbon

Satin (0289) 2 strands **Middle**

Chain (026)

Long and short (040) 3 strands

Outline (0306)

(Actual size)

Use 4 strands of floss unless otherwise noted.

2 strands

Satin (0131)
Straight (0861)

Outline (0861)

Straight (046)

Satin (075) 2 strands

Satin (0289) 2 strands

Long and short (0131) 3 strands

Ribbon around collar (White)

Long and short (White) 3 strands

Satin (0131) 3 strands

Lazy daisy

(0861)
(0167)

Fly (026) 2 strands

Outline filling (075)

Straight

Outline 3 strands

Fly

Outline (075)

Straight (0861)

Open buttonhole (0131)

Satin (0167) 2 strands

Satin (0289) 2 strands **Right**

Chain (040)

Long and short (026)

Satin (0131)
Coral } (0131) 3 strands

Satin (0131) 2 strands

Straight (0861) 2 strands

Outline (0306)

Outline (0861)

Open buttonhole (0167)

Straight

(046) { Lazy daisy

Outline

Coral (040)

Long and short (White) 3 strands

Outline

Outline (0861)

Fly } (0167)

Satin } 2 strands

Outline { (0861)
(0131)

Coral (0131) 3 strands

Satin (White) 2 strands

43

Bridal Gifts

Cards★Instructions on page 46.

Miniature Cushions and Miniature Frames★Instructions on pages 83 and 46.

Cards   shown on page 44

You'll need:
Fabric
Zweigart Art 3882 KLOSTERN, 10 cm (3⁷/₈″)
square, off-white for left, sevres blue for right.
Thread
Anchor 6 strand embroidery floss;
Left
cardinal (020), Flame (0333, 0334), old rose
(078), muscat green (0924, 0281, 0279, 0278),
mustard (0907) and stone (0889) small amount
of each.

Right
sea blue (0978), cornflower (0146), lilac (0107,
0105), stone (0889), jade (0187, 0186), parrot
green (0258), muscat green (0279) and emerald (0923) small amount of each.
Fitting
Colored drawing paper, 22 cm × 11 cm (8⁵/₈″
× 5″⁷/₈″), poppy for left, emerald for right.
Finished size
15 cm × 11 cm (5⁷/₈″ × 4³/₈″).
Directions
Follow directions for Cards on page 2.

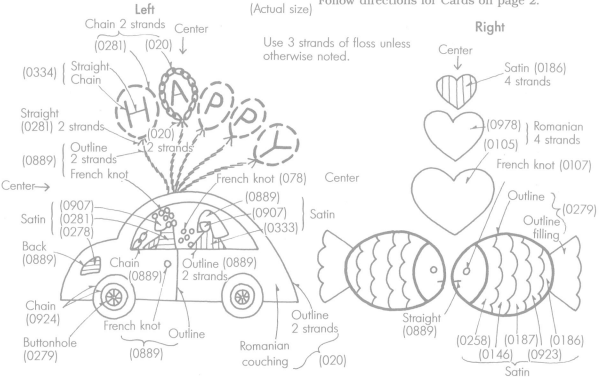

Miniature Frames   shown on page 45

Left Frame
You'll need:
Fabric
Zweigart Art 3711 ARIOSA, soft pink, 20 cm
× 16 cm (7⁷/₈″ × 6¹/₄″).
Thread
Anchor 6 strand embroidery floss;
rose pink (050), laurel green (0206), forest
green (0216), amber gold (0305), golden tan
(0365), carnation (026), sea blue (0978), corn-
flower (0144) and white small amount of each.
Fitting
Frame, 13.5 cm × 9.5 cm (5¹/₄″ × 3³/₄″) inner
size.
Finished size
Same as frame size.

Directions
Match centers of fabric and pattern; copy pat-
tern and embroider.
Frame completed embroidery.

Right frame
You'll need:
Fabric
Zweigart Art 3711 ARIOSA, beige, 20 cm
× 16 cm (7⁷/₈″ × 6¹/₄″).
Thread
Anchor 6 strand embroidery floss;
buttercup (0297), apple green (0203), orange
(0323), golden tan (0365), violet (096), cornflower (0144) and rose pink (050) small amount
of each.

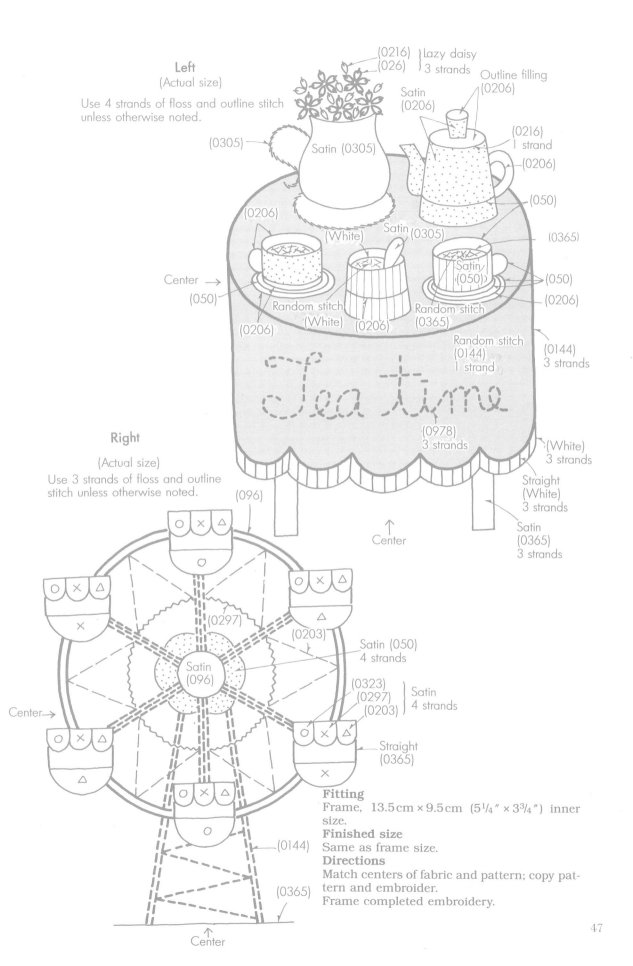

Left

(Actual size)

Use 4 strands of floss and outline stitch unless otherwise noted.

(0216)
(026) } Lazy daisy 3 strands

Outline filling (0206)

Satin (0206)

(0216) 1 strand

(0206)

(0305)

Satin (0305)

(050)

(0206)

(White)

Satin (0305)

(0365)

Satin (050)

(050)

Center →

(050)

(0206)

Random stitch (White)

(0206)

Random stitch (0365)

(0206)

Random stitch (0144) 1 strand

(0144) 3 strands

Tea time

(0978) 3 strands

(White) 3 strands

Straight (White) 3 strands

Satin (0365) 3 strands

↑ Center

Right

(Actual size)

Use 3 strands of floss and outline stitch unless otherwise noted.

(096)

(0297)

(0203)

Satin (050) 4 strands

Satin (096)

(0323)
(0297)
(0203) } Satin 4 strands

Straight (0365)

Center →

(0144)

(0365)

↑ Center

Fitting

Frame, 13.5 cm × 9.5 cm (5¼″ × 3¾″) inner size.

Finished size

Same as frame size.

Directions

Match centers of fabric and pattern; copy pattern and embroider.

Frame completed embroidery.

47

Teapot cover(A), Potholders(B, C), Coasters(D, E, F, G) and Jar Covers(H, I)

Potholders (B, C)

shown on pages 48–49

You'll need:
Fabric
B···White terrycloth, green heavy cotton cloth and flannel, 16 cm × 20 cm (6¼″ × 7⅞″) each, green checkered fabric, 50 cm square (19⅝″).

C···parma violet terrycloth, pink heavy cotton cloth and flannel, 16 cm × 20 cm (6¼″ × 7⅞″) each, pink-on-white polka-dotted fabric, 50 cm (19⅝″) square.

B

(Actual size)

Front piece···Terrycloth
Back piece···Cotton cloth
Padding···Flannel
} 1 piece each

Same for B and C

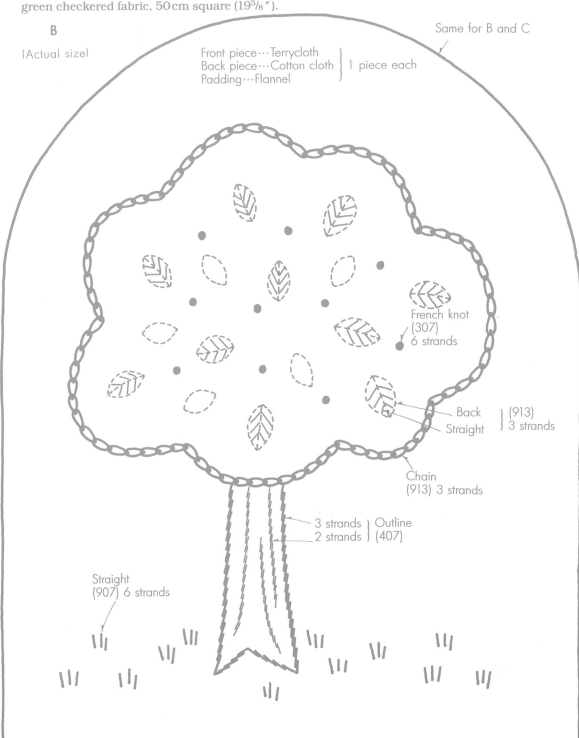

French knot
(307)
6 strands

Back
Straight
} (913)
3 strands

Chain
(913) 3 strands

3 strands
2 strands
} Outline
(407)

Straight
(907) 6 strands

50

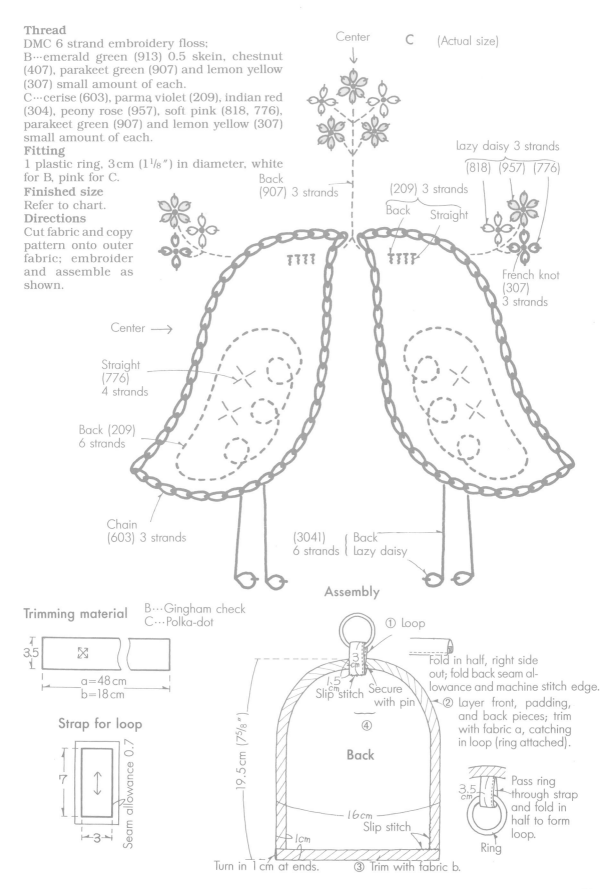

Thread

DMC 6 strand embroidery floss;

B···emerald green (913) 0.5 skein, chestnut (407), parakeet green (907) and lemon yellow (307) small amount of each.

C···cerise (603), parma violet (209), indian red (304), peony rose (957), soft pink (818, 776), parakeet green (907) and lemon yellow (307) small amount of each.

Fitting

1 plastic ring, 3 cm ($1\frac{1}{8}$″) in diameter, white for B, pink for C.

Finished size

Refer to chart.

Directions

Cut fabric and copy pattern onto outer fabric; embroider and assemble as shown.

Center   C   (Actual size)

Back (907) 3 strands

Lazy daisy 3 strands
(818) (957) (776)

(209) 3 strands

Back   Straight

French knot (307) 3 strands

Center →

Straight (776) 4 strands

Back (209) 6 strands

Chain (603) 3 strands

(3041) 6 strands { Back / Lazy daisy

Assembly

Trimming material   B···Gingham check
C···Polka-dot

3.5
a=48 cm
b=18 cm

Strap for loop

7
3
Seam allowance 0.7

① Loop

Fold in half, right side out; fold back seam allowance and machine stitch edge.

3 cm

1.5 cm
Slip stitch   Secure with pin

② Layer front, padding, and back pieces; trim with fabric a, catching in loop (ring attached).

④

Back

19.5 cm ($7\frac{5}{8}$″)

3.5 cm   Pass ring through strap and fold in half to form loop.

Ring

16 cm

Slip stitch

1 cm

Turn in 1 cm at ends.   ③ Trim with fabric b.

51

Apron ★ Instructions on page 89.

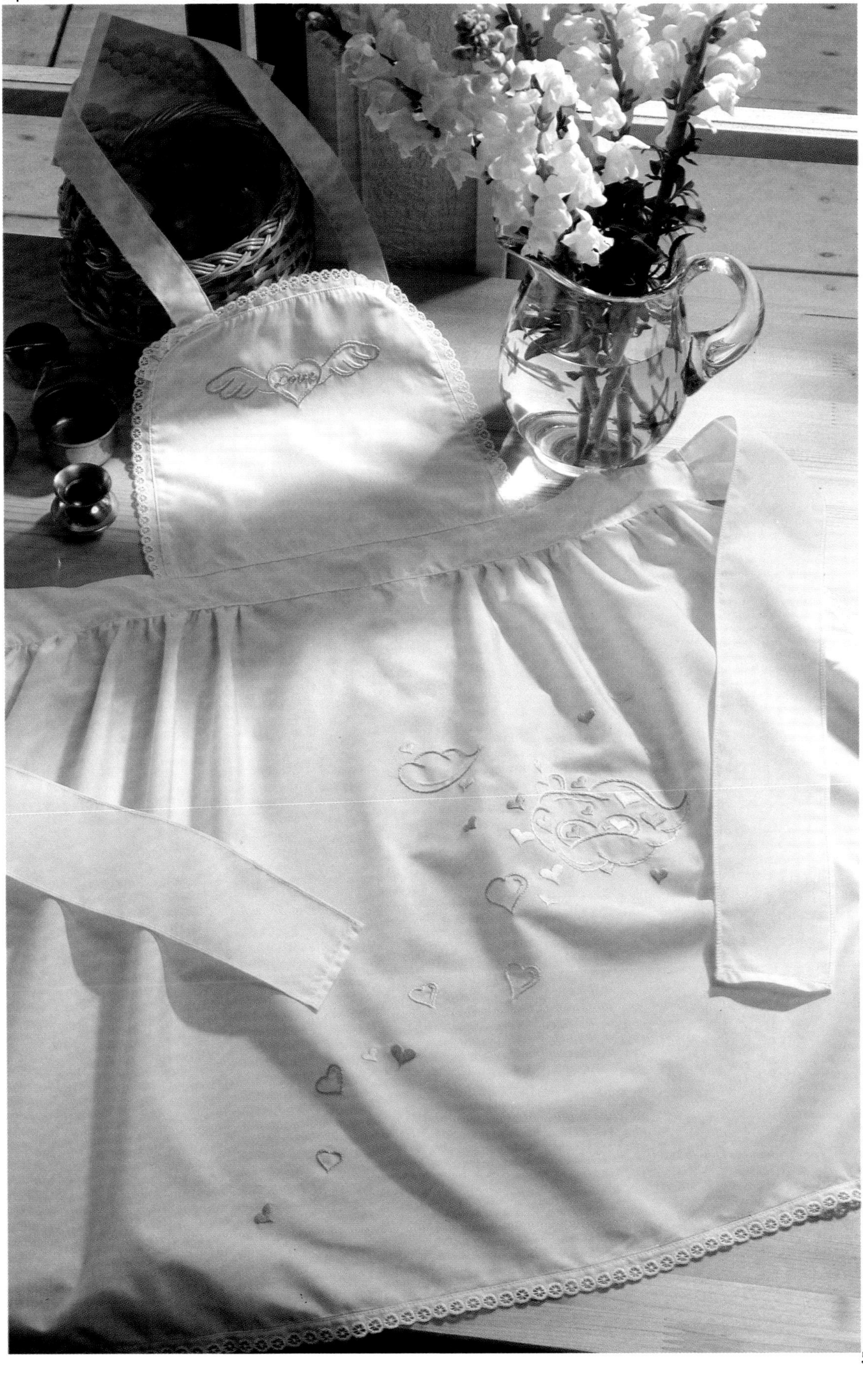

Luncheon Mats   shown on page 52

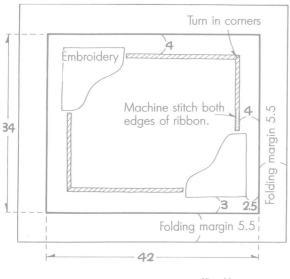

Turn in corners

Embroidery

4

Machine stitch both
edges of ribbon.

4

34

Folding margin 5.5

3   2.5

Folding margin 5.5

42

(Back)

Fold back margin and slip stitch

4.5 cm

1cm

4.5cm

Miter corners

You'll need:
Fabric (for 1 mat)
Zweigart Art 3711 ARIOSA, white, 53cm ×
45cm (20⁷/₈″ × 17³/₄″).
Thread
Anchor 6 strand embroidery floss;
Top Mat···moss green (0266) 0.5 skein, rose
pink (054, 052, 050), forest green (0216, 0214),
moss green (0268), golden tan (0365), cyclamen (087, 086), gorse yellow (0303) and cardinal (042) small amount of each.
Lower Mat···moss green (0266) 0.5 skein, amber gold (0305), gorse yellow (0301, 0303),
muscat green (0925), cobalt blue (0130, 0129),
forest green (0216, 0214), moss green (0268)
and golden tan (0365) small amount of each.
Fitting
Satin ribbon, 0.6cm (¹/₄″) in width, 80cm
(31¹/₂″) length, soft pink for top mat, canary
yellow for lower.
Finished size
42cm × 34cm (16¹/₂″ × 13³/₈″).
Directions
Copy pattern onto fabric and embroider. Sew
on ribbon and trim edges.

Use 4 strands of floss unless
otherwise noted.

(Actual size) Numbers inside parenthesis
for top mat; those in brackets
for bottom.

a = (087) [0130]
b = (086) [0129]   } Satin
x = [(0216)]   3 strands

Long and short
Use 3 strands of floss
for inner part of petal.

(054)   (050)   (052)   (042)
[0303] [0301] [0305] [0925]

Long and short { [(0268)]
                         [(0266)]

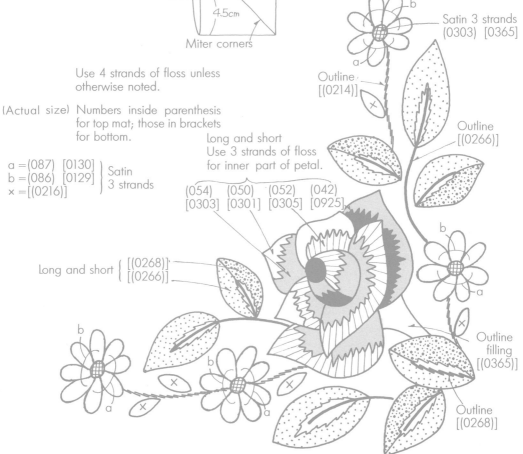

Satin 3 strands
(0303) [0365]

Outline
[(0214)]

Outline
[(0266)]

Outline
filling
[(0365)]

Outline
[(0268)]

Napkins

You'll need:
Fabric (for 1 napkin)
Zweigart Art 3711 ARIOSA, white,
37 cm (14½″) square.
Thread
Anchor 6 strand embroidery floss;
Left⋯cobalt blue (0130, 0129, 0128),
forest green (0126, 0214), moss green
(0266, 0264), gorse yellow (0302, 0301)
and raspberry (068, 066) small amount
of each.
Right⋯raspberry (068, 066), cyclamen
(085), forest green (0216, 0214), moss
green (0266, 0264), gorse yellow (0302,
0301) and cobalt blue (0130, 0129) small
amount of each.
Fitting (for 1 napkin).
Trimming tape, 1 cm (³⁄₈″) in width,
145 cm (57⅛″) length.
Finished size
36.5 cm square (14³⁄₈″).
Directions
Copy pattern onto corner of fabric and
embroider; finish napkins as shown.

Assembly

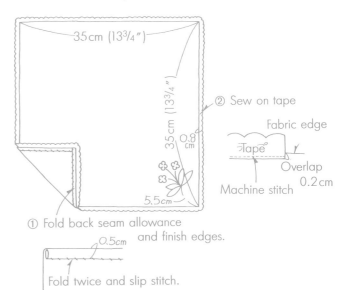

① Fold back seam allowance
and finish edges.

Fold twice and slip stitch.

② Sew on tape

Fabric edge
Tape
Overlap
0.2 cm
Machine stitch

(Actual size) Use 3 strands of floss.

Numbers inside parenthesis for left napkin;
those in brackets for right.

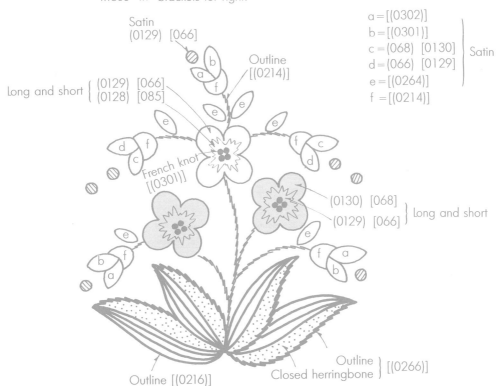

Satin
(0129) [066]

Outline
[(0214)]

Long and short { (0129) [066]
                (0128) [085]

French knot
[(0301)]

a = [(0302)]
b = [(0301)]
c = (068) [0130] } Satin
d = (066) [0129]
e = [(0264)]
f = [(0214)]

(0130) [068]
(0129) [066] } Long and short

Outline [(0216)]
Closed herringbone }
Outline } [(0266)]

55

Cards ★Instructions on page 58.

Lovely Presents

Coasters and Doilies★Instructions on pages 59(A, B), 94(C, D, E) and 95(F, G).

Cards   *shown on page 56*

You'll need:
Fabric
Zweigart Art 3882 KLOSTERN, 10cm (3⁷/₈″) square, off-white for top card, purple for lower.
Thread
Anchor 6 srand embroidery floss;
Top···moss green (0268, 0267), mustard (0907), muscat green (0281, 0279, 0924), old rose (065), cardinal (020), flame (0334) and maize (0944) small amount of each, bits of gold lamé thread.

Lower···cyclamen (087, 088), violet (0107, 098), muscat green (0281, 0924) and mustard (0907) small amount of each.
Fitting
Colored drawing paper, 22cm × 15cm (8⁵/₈″ × 5⁷/₈″), red for top, episcopal purple for lower.
Finished size
15cm × 11cm (5⁷/₈″ × 4³/₈″).
Directions
See directions for Card on page 2.

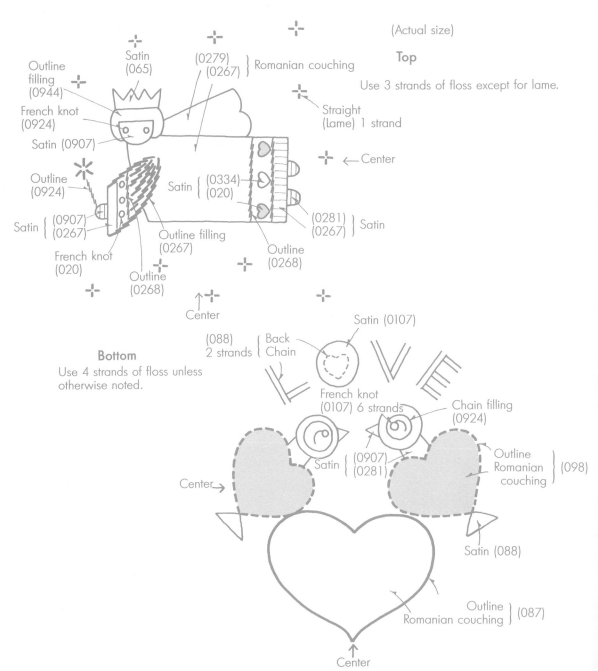

Coasters (A, B)   *shown on page 57*

You'll need:

Fabric

Zweigart Art 3609 BELFAST, A⋯sky blue 24 cm × 12 cm (9½″ × 4¾″), white 12 cm × 4 cm (4¾″ × 1⅝″); B⋯beige brown 24 cm × 12 cm (9½″ × 4¾″) cornflower blue 12 cm × 4 cm (4¾″ × 1⅝″).

Thread

Anchor 6 strand embroidery floss;

A⋯coffee (0905), linen (0932), ecru (0926), canary yellow (0288), maize (0944), haze (0922), gorse yellow (0300), cream (0386), canary yellow (0290), moss green (0264), forest green (0216, 0214) and white small smount of each.

B⋯navy blur (0152), parma violet (0108), mauve (0869), mist green (0859), gray (0401), dusky pink (0895), carnation (023), moss green (0264), linen (0391), coffee (0905), lilac (0105) and white small amount of each.

Finished size

11 cm square (4⅜″).

Directions

Copy pattern and embroider after patching together outer fabrics ⓐ and ⓑ.

Sew on clouds. Sew together front and back pieces, right sides facing, leaving opening for turning out. Turn out to right side and close opening. Machine stitch around edges to finish.

(Actual size)

Use 2 strands of floss.
Satin stitch unless otherwise noted.
Numbers inside parenthesis for A;
those in brackets for B

Add 0.5 cm seam allowance on all pieces.

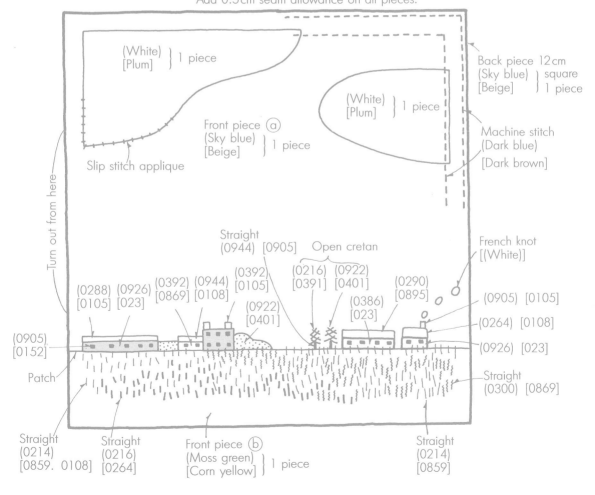

Table Mat shown on page 60

You'll need:

Fabric

Light cream cotton cloth, 36 cm × 29 cm (14$\frac{1}{8}$″ × 11$\frac{3}{8}$″).

Thread

Anchor 6 strand embroidery floss; cyclamen (087, 086, 085), violet (095), laurel green (0208), amber gold (0305), turquoise (0928), carnation (026) and moss green (0265) small amount of each.

Fitting

Canary yellow tape, 1.2 cm ($\frac{1}{2}$″) width, 140 cm (55$\frac{1}{8}$″) length. 20 pink round beads (small).

Finished size

36 cm × 29 cm (14$\frac{1}{8}$″ × 11$\frac{3}{8}$″).

Directions

Copy pattern onto fabric and embroider; trim edges with bias tape.

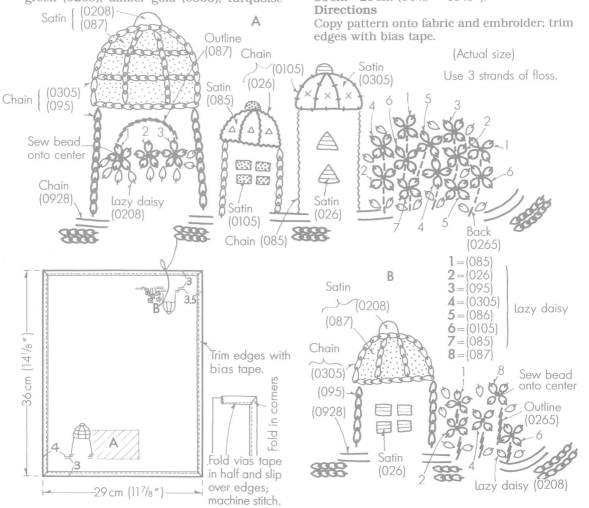

(Actual size)

Use 3 strands of floss.

Satin { (0208) (087)

Outline (087)

Chain (026)

(0105)

Satin (085)

A

Satin (0305)

Chain { (0305) (095)

Sew bead onto center

Chain (0928)

Lazy daisy (0208)

Satin (0105)

Chain (085)

Satin (026)

Back (0265)

1 = (085)
2 = (026)
3 = (095)
4 = (0305)
5 = (086)
6 = (0105)
7 = (085)
8 = (087)

Lazy daisy

36 cm (14$\frac{1}{8}$″)

Trim edges with bias tape.

Fold in corners

Fold vias tape in half and slip over edges; machine stitch.

B

A

29 cm (11$\frac{7}{8}$″)

Satin (0208)

(087)

Chain (0305)

(095)

(0928)

Satin (026)

Sew bead onto center

Outline (0265)

Lazy daisy (0208)

Miniature Frames shown on page 60

Right frame

You'll need:

Fabric

(Light) Soft pink cotton cloth, 17 cm (6$\frac{3}{4}$″) square.

Thread

Anchor 6 strand embroidery floss; cyclamen (087, 085), strawberry (0968), violet (098), carnation (027), geranium (06), cream (0386), amber gold (0305), moss green (0265) and laurel green (0208) small amount of each.

Fitting

12 pink round beads (small). Frame, 11 cm (4$\frac{3}{8}$″) square in inner size.

Finished size

Same as frame size.

Directions

Copy pattern onto fabric and embroider; frame when completed.

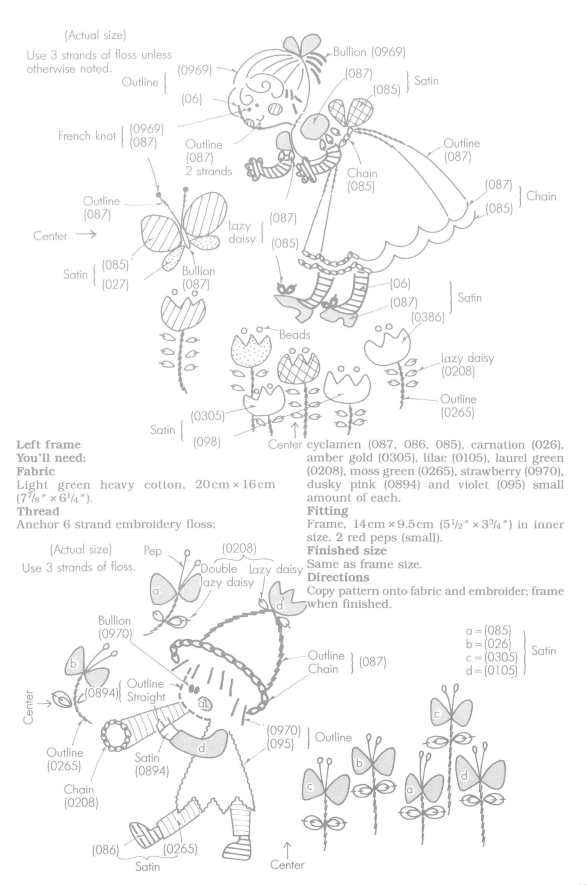

(Actual size)

Use 3 strands of floss unless otherwise noted.

Outline { (0969) / (06)

Bullion (0969)

(087)
(085) } Satin

French knot { (0969) / (087)

Outline (087) 2 strands

Outline (087)

Center →

Outline (087)

Satin { (085) / (027)

Bullion (087)

Lazy daisy { (087) / (085)

Chain (085)

Outline (087)

(087)
(085) } Chain

(06)
(087)
(0386) } Satin

Beads

Lazy daisy (0208)

Outline (0265)

Satin { (0305) / (098)

Center

Left frame
You'll need:
Fabric
Light green heavy cotton, 20 cm × 16 cm (7⁷/₈″ × 6¹/₄″).
Thread
Anchor 6 strand embroidery floss;

cyclamen (087, 086, 085), carnation (026), amber gold (0305), lilac (0105), laurel green (0208), moss green (0265), strawberry (0970), dusky pink (0894) and violet (095) small amount of each.
Fitting
Frame, 14 cm × 9.5 cm (5¹/₂″ × 3³/₄″) in inner size. 2 red peps (small).
Finished size
Same as frame size.
Directions
Copy pattern onto fabric and embroider; frame when finished.

(Actual size)
Use 3 strands of floss.

Pep

(0208)

Double lazy daisy

Lazy daisy

Bullion (0970)

Outline Chain } (087)

Outline Straight

(0894) {

Center →

Outline (0265)

Chain (0208)

Satin (0894)

(0970)
(095) } Outline

(086) / (0265)
Satin

Center

a = (085)
b = (026)
c = (0305)
d = (0105) } Satin

Table Runner shown on page 64

(Actual size)
Use 3 strands of floss unless
otherwise noted.

Back 6 strands
(040)   Center   (010)

○ =(076)
◐ =(040) } French knot
● =(White)

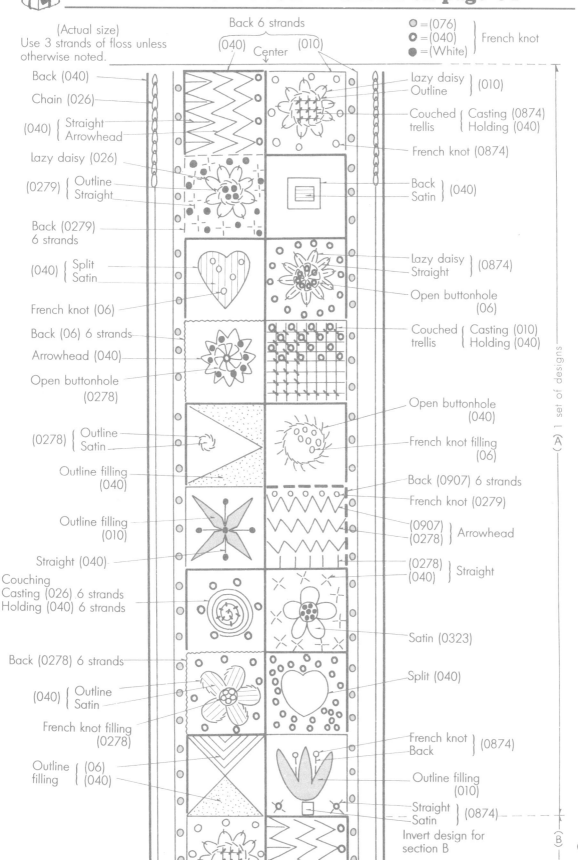

Back (040)

Chain (026)

(040) { Straight
Arrowhead

Lazy daisy (026)

(0279) { Outline
Straight

Back (0279)
6 strands

(040) { Split
Satin

French knot (06)

Back (06) 6 strands

Arrowhead (040)

Open buttonhole
(0278)

(0278) { Outline
Satin

Outline filling
(040)

Outline filling
(010)

Straight (040)

Couching
Casting (026) 6 strands
Holding (040) 6 strands

Back (0278) 6 strands

(040) { Outline
Satin

French knot filling
(0278)

Outline { (06)
filling { (040)

Lazy daisy } (010)
Outline

Couched { Casting (0874)
trellis { Holding (040)

French knot (0874)

Back } (040)
Satin

Lazy daisy } (0874)
Straight

Open buttonhole
(06)

Couched { Casting (010)
trellis { Holding (040)

Open buttonhole
(040)

French knot filling
(06)

Back (0907) 6 strands

French knot (0279)

(0907) } Arrowhead
(0278)

(0278) } Straight
(040)

Satin (0323)

Split (040)

French knot } (0874)
Back

Outline filling
(010)

Straight } (0874)
Satin

Invert design for
section B

(A) 1 set of designs

(B)

65

You'll need:
Fabric
Zweigart Art 3609 BELFAST, unbleached, 68 cm × 24 cm (26³/₄″ × 9¹/₂″).
Thread
Anchor 6 strand embroidery floss; cardinal (040), geranium (010, 06), carnation (026), old rose (076), muscat green (0278, 0279), mustard (0907, 0874), orange (0323) and white small amount of each.
Finished size
75 cm × 18 cm (29¹/₂″ × 7¹/₁₆″).
Directions
Copy pattern onto fabric and embroider; finish seam allowance as shown and attach tassels.

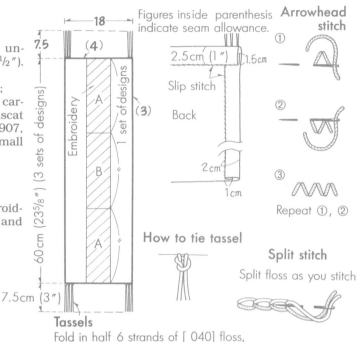

Figures inside parenthesis indicate seam allowance.

Arrowhead stitch

① ② ③
Repeat ①, ②

Slip stitch
Back

How to tie tassel

Split stitch
Split floss as you stitch

Tassels
Fold in half 6 strands of [040] floss, 16 cm in length; make 54 tassels.

Handkerchieves   shown on page 8

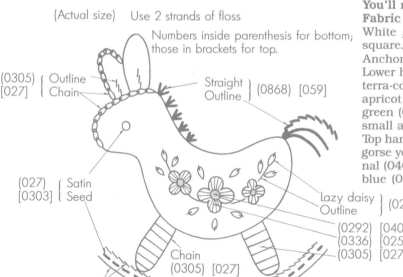

(Actual size)   Use 2 strands of floss

Numbers inside parenthesis for bottom; those in brackets for top.

(0305) [027] } Outline / Chain

Straight } (0868) [059] Outline

(027) [0303] } Satin / Seed

Chain (0305) [027]

Outline [(0167)]

Lazy daisy Outline } (0208) [0265]

(0292) [040]
(0336) [025] } Satin
(0305) [027]

You'll need:
Fabric
White gauze handkerchief, 32 cm square. (13″) **Thread**
Anchor 6 strand embroidery floss;
Lower hadkerchief–amber gold (0305), terra-cotta (0336), buttercup (0292), apricot (0868), carnation (027), laurel green (0208) and peacock blue (0167) small amount of each.
Top handkerchief–carnation (027, 025), gorse yellow (0303) red pink (059) cardinal (040), moss green (0265) peacock blue (0167) small amount of each.

Towel Trains   shown on page 9

You'll need:
Fabric
Cotton terrycloth–Left: sky blue, 20 cm (7⁷/₈″) square, ivory, 34 cm × 12 cm (13³/₈″ × 4³/₄″), biege, 20 cm × 15 cm (7⁷/₈″ × 5⁷/₈″).
Right: soft pink, 20 cm square (7⁷/₈″), ivory, 34 cm × 12 cm (13³/₈″ × 4³/₄″), beige, 20 cm × 15 cm (7⁷/₈″ × 5⁷/₈″).
Thread
DMC 6 strand embroidery floss;

Left–geranium pink (894), royal blue (996), emerald green (954), saffron (727) and chestnut (407) small amount of each.
Right–soft pink (899), emerald green (954), saffron (727), sevres blue (798) and chestnut (407) small amount of each.
Fitting
Fiberfill.
Finished size
Refer to chart.

Directions

Cut fabric to size; copy patterns onto both A and B pieces and embroider.

For train A, match side and width pieces, right sides facing so that opening for stuffing comes to bottom; sew pieces together, leaving bottom open. For train B, sew top, bottom, and side pieces, right sides facing, leaving opening for stuffing; turn right-side-out and stuff both A and B; close opening.

Run gathering stitches around wheel; pull fabric closed over stuffing and sew wheels onto trains; prepare connecting "chain" by knitting threads. Attach A and B trains to finish.

Pattern (Actual size)

Use 3 strands of floss unless otherwise noted.

Add 1 cm seam allowance for all pieces.

Numbers inside parenthesis for left; those in brackets for right.

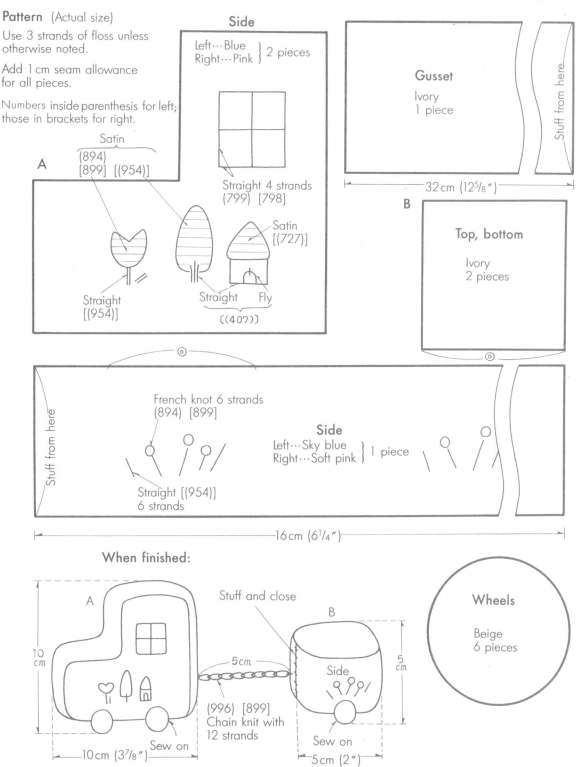

Side
Left···Blue
Right···Pink } 2 pieces

A

Satin
(894)
[899] [(954)]

Straight 4 strands
(799) [798]

Satin
[(727)]

Straight
[(954)]

Straight   Fly
((407))

Gusset
Ivory
1 piece

Stuff from here

32cm (12⁵/₈")

B

Top, bottom
Ivory
2 pieces

Stuff from here

French knot 6 strands
(894) [899]

Side
Left···Sky blue
Right···Soft pink } 1 piece

Straight [(954)]
6 strands

16cm (6¹/₄")

When finished:

A

Stuff and close

B

Wheels
Beige
6 pieces

10 cm

5cm

Side

5 cm

(996) [899]
Chain knit with
12 strands

10cm (3⁷/₈")   Sew on

Sew on

5cm (2")

67

🎁 Pillow Case, Blanket Guard   shown on page 9

Pillow Case

Front
Embroidery (Set patterns symmetrically)

Seam allowance 1

36 cm (14 1/8")

27 cm (10 5/8")

Front
Selvage

Seam allowance 1

32 cm (12 5/8")

27

Selvage

Back
Selvage

Seam allowance 1

14 cm (5 1/2")

Frills   2 pieces
Seam allowance 1

86 cm (33 7/8")

6 cm (2 3/8")

(Actual size) Use 2 strands of floss.

Finished line

Outline
(0305)

Long and Short

Outline

Satin
(0401)

Straight
(0303)

(025)
(0208) } Satin

Outline
(0208)

Overlap 10 cm

Front

Back

Frill

Lace

7 cm

Sew frill and lace on at an angle; cut off excess material.

Assembly

② Sew front and back pieces together; right sides facing, catching in frill and ruffled lace; turn out.

Frill

Frill

Lace

3 cm

① Patch together frill pieces; finish edges on one side and ruffle with gathering stitches.

Frill

Back

Seam allowance

0.5 cm

Gathering stitch

68

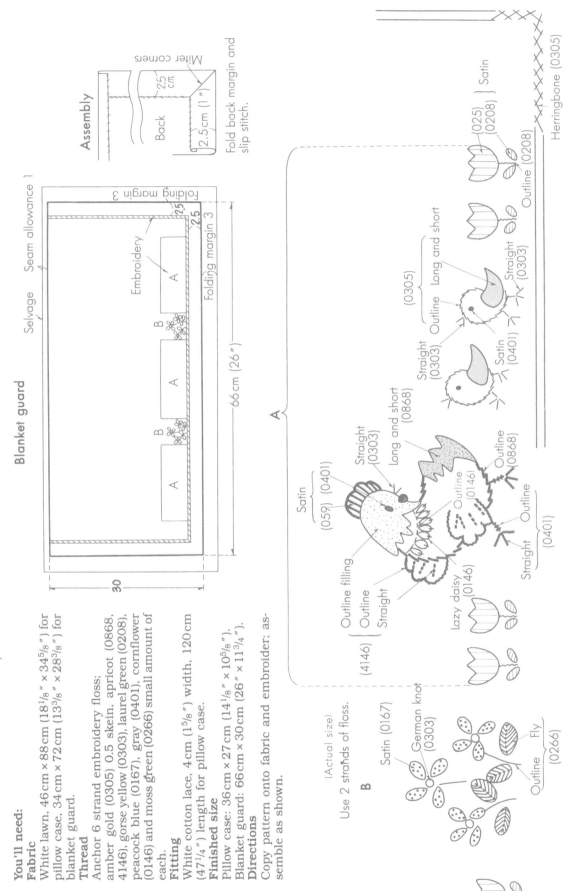

Blanket guard

Assembly

Miter corners

Back

2.5 cm

2.5 cm (1")

Fold back margin and slip stitch.

Selvage   Seam allowance 1

Folding margin 3

Embroidery

2.5

2.5

A   B   A   B   A

66 cm (26")

Folding margin 3

30

You'll need:

Fabric

White lawn, 46 cm × 88 cm (18¹/₈" × 34⁵/₈") for pillow case, 34 cm × 72 cm (13³/₈" × 28³/₈") for blanket guard.

Thread

Anchor 6 strand embroidery floss; amber gold (0305) 0.5 skein, apricot (0868, 4146), gorse yellow (0303), laurel green (0208), peacock blue (0167), gray (0401), cornflower (0146) and moss green (0266) small amount of each.

Fitting

White cotton lace, 4 cm (1⁵/₈") width, 120 cm (47¹/₄") length for pillow case.

Finished size

Pillow case: 36 cm × 27 cm (14¹/₈" × 10⁵/₈").
Blanket guard: 66 cm × 30 cm (26" × 11³/₄").

Directions

Copy pattern onto fabric and embroider; assemble as shown.

(Actual size)

Use 2 strands of floss.

A

Satin (059) (0401)

Straight (0303)

Long and short (0868)

Outline (0868)

Outline (0146)

Straight

Outline filling (4146)

Outline

Lazy daisy (0146)

Straight Outline (0401)

Outline (0303) Long and short

Straight (0303)

Satin (0401)

Straight (0303)

Satin (025) (0208)

Outline (0208)

Herringbone (0305)

B

Satin (0167)

German knot (0303)

Outline   Fly (0266)

Album
shown on pages 12–13

You'll need:

Fabric
Zweigart Art 3711 ARIOSA, soft pink, 75cm × 44cm (29¼″ × 17⅜″).

Thread
Anchor 6 strand embroidery floss; old rose (076), carnation (026), canary yellow (0291), kingfisher (0160) 0.5 skein each.
cinnamon (0367), gray (0400) and white small amount of each.

Finished size
34cm × 30cm (13⅜″ × 11¾″).

Directions
Embroider as shown in diagram.
You may require professional help to have embroidery fitted onto album.

(Actual size) Use 4 strands of floss.
Outline stitch unless otherwise noted.

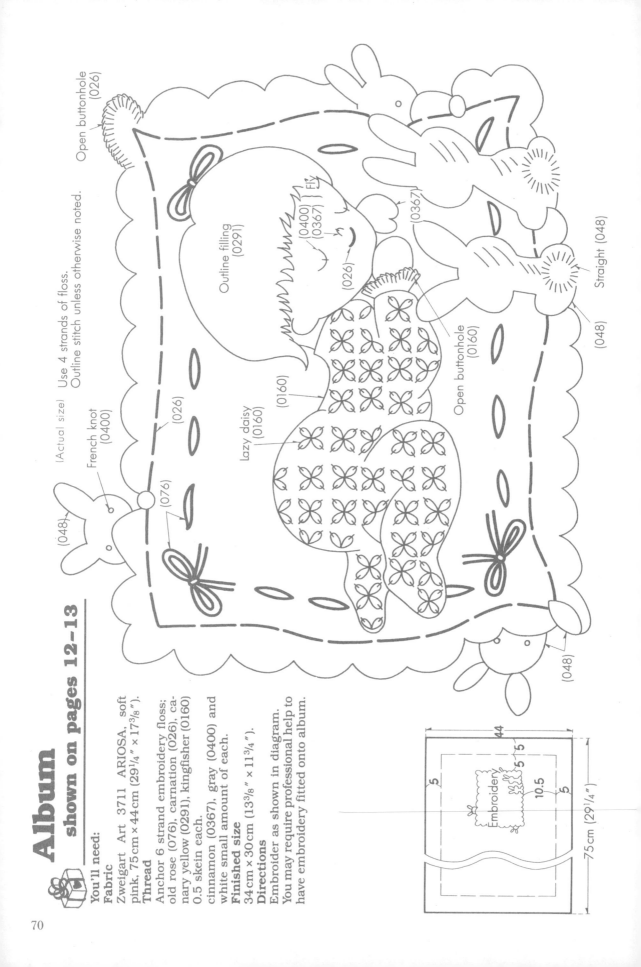

Open buttonhole (026)

French knot (0400)

(048)

(076)

(026)

Outline filling (0291)

(0400) (0367) } Fly

(026)

(0160)

Lazy daisy (0160)

(0367)

(0367)

Open buttonhole (0160)

Straight (048)

(048)

(048)

Embroidery

44

5 5

5 5

10.5

5

5

75cm (29¼″)

34cm (13⅜″)

Cards shown on page 16

You'll need:
Fabric
Broadcloth, 11 cm × 9 cm (4³/₈″ × 3¹/₂″), yellow for top card, pink for bottom.
Thread
Anchor 6 strand embroidery floss;
Top card-carnation (029) flame (0335) grass green (0242) lido blue (0433) lilac (0107) emerald (0227) rasberry (068) tangerine (0314) navy blue (0149) haze (0920) golden tan (0365) and peat brown (0381) small amount of each.
Bottom card-lilac (0107), raspberry (068), carnation (029), gorse yellow (0303), buttercup (0295), lido blue (0433), peat brown (0381) and white small amount of each.
Fitting
Top card-Tangerine yellow drawing paper, 18 cm × 30 cm (7¹/₁₆″ × 11³/₄″).
White cotton lace, 1.5 cm (⁵/₈″) width, 50 cm (19⁵/₈″) length.
Tirolian tape, 1.5 cm (⁵/₈″) width, 45 cm (17³/₄″) length.
Bottom card-Lemon yellow drawing paper, 18 cm × 26 cm (7¹/₁₆″ × 10¹/₄″).
White nylon lace, 1.5 cm (⁵/₈″) width, 50 cm (19⁵/₈″) length.
Braid flower ribbon, 1.5 cm (⁵/₈″) width, 30 cm (11³/₄″) length.
Finished size
18 cm × 15 cm (7¹/₁₆″ × 5⁷/₈″) for top card;
18 cm × 13 cm (7¹/₁₆″ × 5¹/₈″) for bottom.

Top

(Actual size) Use 2 strands of floss
Outline stitch unless otherwise noted.

Directions
Top card-copy pattern onto fabric and embroider. Sew on lace and Tirolian tape as shown; glue onto card.
Bottom card-copy pattern onto fabric and embroider; cut into oval and glue onto card. Ruffle lace with gathering stitches and glue onto card. Decorate with braid flowers.

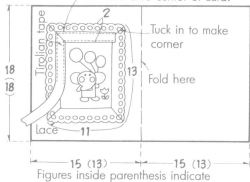

Machine stitch together and blue onto center of card.

Figures inside parenthesis indicate measurements for bottom card.

Bottom

Use 2 strands of floss unless otherwise noted.

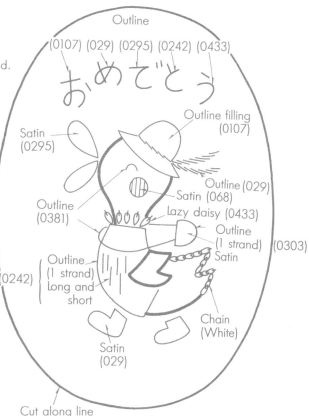

Pochettes (A) shown on page 20

(Actual size) Add 1 cm seam allowance when cutting.

You'll need:
Fabric
Saffron heavy cotton cloth, 71 cm × 27 cm (28″ × 10⅝″).
Cotton lining fabric, 44 cm × 22 cm (17⅜″ × 8⅝″).
Thread
Anchor 6 strand embroidery floss;
carnation (024), moss green(0266) and white small amount of each.
Fitting
Cream cotton lace, 3 cm (1⅛″) width, 150 cm (50″) length.

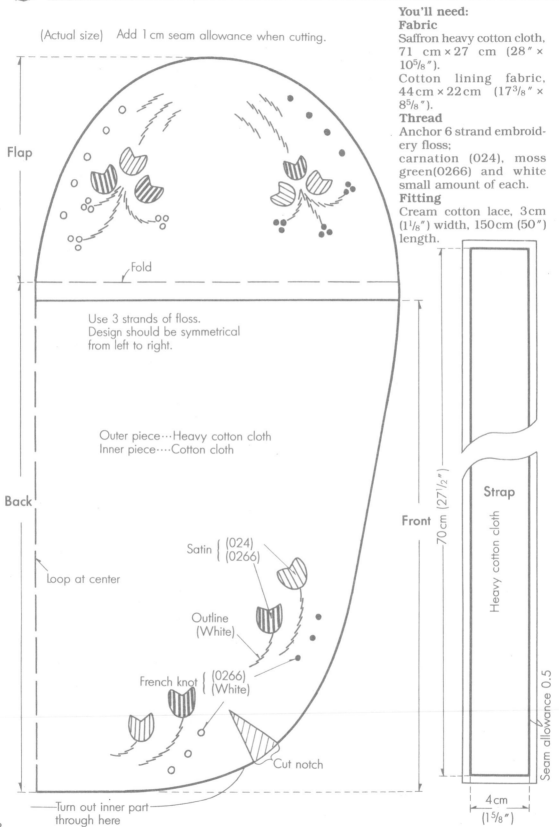

Flap

Fold

Use 3 strands of floss.
Design should be symmetrical
from left to right.

Outer piece···Heavy cotton cloth
Inner piece····Cotton cloth

Back

Loop at center

Satin { (024)
        (0266)

Outline
(White)

French knot { (0266)
             (White)

Turn out inner part
through here

Cut notch

Front

70 cm (27½″)

Strap

Heavy cotton cloth

Seam allowance 0.5

4cm
(1⅝″)

72

Velcro, 2.5 cm (1″) width, 5 cm (2″) length.
Finished size
Refer to chart.
Directions
Cut fabric···back and flap sections should be one piece.
Copy patterns onto flap and front sections; embroider and assemble as shown.

④ Match 2 and 3, right sides facing, and sew mouth.

⑦ Cut out round pieces of Velcro; sew onto front piece and underside of flap and.

⑥ Sew strap and attach to back piece.

Assembly

2cm

Fold back seam allowance and machine stitch edges.

Fold
2cm
2cm
Back
13.5 cm
2cm Lace
20 cm

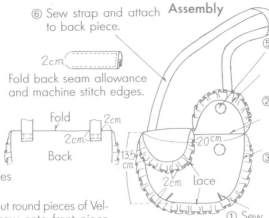

⑤ Ruffle 40 cm of lace; sew flap pieces together, catching in lace; turn right-side-out and close opening.

② Ruffle 70 cm of lace; sew front and back outer pieces together, right sides facing and catching in lace.

③ Sew notches closed for inner pieces; sew front and back pieces together, leaving opening for turning out.

① Sew notches closed for front and back outer pieces.

Pin Cushions (D, E)   shown on pages 32–33

You'll need:
Fabric
(for one cushion).
Zweigart Art 3609 BELFAST, white, 22 cm × 11 cm (8⅝″ × 4⅜″).
Thread
Anchor 6 strand embroidery floss;
D···cornflower (0148), sea blue (0978), kingfisher (0158, 0160), slate gray (0900) and white small amount of each.
E···old rose (078), carnation (026, 025), slate

gray (0900) and white small amount of each.
Fitting
White cotton lace, 3 cm (1⅛″) width, 60 cm (23⅝″) length (for one).
Ribbon, 0.8 cm (⅜″) width, 80 cm (31½″) length, sevres blue for D, faded pink for E.
Finished size
15 cm (5⅞″) square.
Directions
Copy pattern onto front piece and embroider; assemble as shown.

(Actual size)

Numbers inside parenthesis for D; those in brackets for E.
Satin
(0158) [025] 2 strands

(White)
} Chain 1 strand
(0160) [026]

Satin
Outline } (0900) 2 strands

French knot
(0148) [078] 2 strands

Chain (White) 1 strand

Satin
(0978) [026] 2 strands

Add 0.5 cm seam allowance all around; cut 2 pieces.

Sew pieces together, right sides facing and catching in lace; Stuff with filled inner cushion.

When finished:

15 cm (5⅞″)
15 cm (5⅞″)

Pass ribbon through holes in lace.

Bags (B)

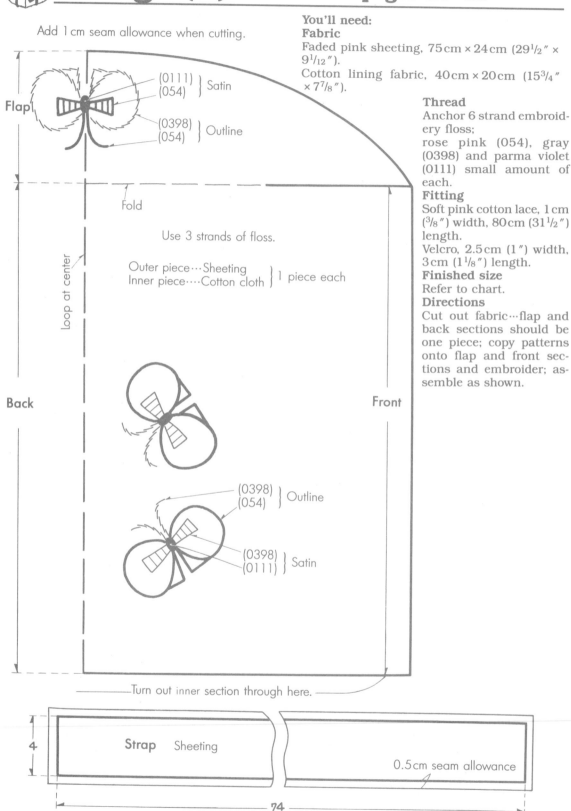

Add 1 cm seam allowance when cutting.

(0111)
(054) } Satin

(0398)
(054) } Outline

Flap

Fold

Loop at center

Use 3 strands of floss.

Outer piece····Sheeting
Inner piece····Cotton cloth } 1 piece each

Back

Front

(0398)
(054) } Outline

(0398)
(0111) } Satin

Turn out inner section through here.

Strap   Sheeting

4

0.5cm seam allowance

74

You'll need:
Fabric
Faded pink sheeting, 75 cm × 24 cm (29$\frac{1}{2}$″ × 9$\frac{1}{12}$″).
Cotton lining fabric, 40 cm × 20 cm (15$\frac{3}{4}$″ × 7$\frac{7}{8}$″).

Thread
Anchor 6 strand embroidery floss;
rose pink (054), gray (0398) and parma violet (0111) small amount of each.
Fitting
Soft pink cotton lace, 1 cm ($\frac{3}{8}$″) width, 80 cm (31$\frac{1}{2}$″) length.
Velcro, 2.5 cm (1″) width, 3 cm (1$\frac{1}{8}$″) length.
Finished size
Refer to chart.
Directions
Cut out fabric····flap and back sections should be one piece; copy patterns onto flap and front sections and embroider; assemble as shown.

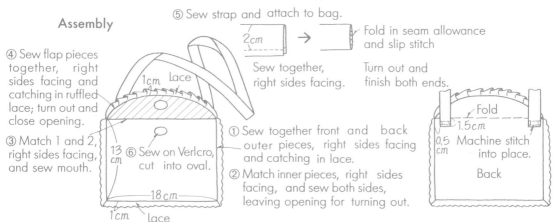

Assembly

Use 2 strands of floss and satin stitch unless otherwise noted.

⑤ Sew strap and attach to bag.

2cm → Fold in seam allowance and slip stitch

Sew together, right sides facing.

Turn out and finish both ends.

④ Sew flap pieces together, right sides facing and catching in ruffled lace; turn out and close opening.

1cm Lace

③ Match 1 and 2, right sides facing, and sew mouth.

13 cm ⑥ Sew on Verlcro, cut into oval.

18 cm

1cm Lace

① Sew together front and back outer pieces, right sides facing and catching in lace.

② Match inner pieces, right sides facing, and sew both sides, leaving opening for turning out.

Fold
1.5 cm
0.5 cm Machine stitch into place.
Back

Brooches   shown on page 36

You'll need:

Fabric

Top brooch···Faded pink broadcloth, 5 cm (2″) square, bits of pink felt.

Bottom brooch···Sevres blue broadcloth, 5 cm (2″) square, bits of light blue felt.

Left brooch···Azure blue broadcloth, 5 cm (2″) square, bits of light blue felt.

Thread

Anchor 6 strand embroidery floss;

Top···cardinal (040), cyclamen (085), orange (0323), terra-cotta (0336), moss green (0266), buttercup (0295) and carnation (026) small amount of each.

Bottom···cornflower (0145), cobalt blue (0129), buttercup (0295), carnation (024, 026), moss green (0266), lilac (0105) and violet (095) small amount of each.

Left···violet (095, 094), carnation (026), corn flower (0145), cobalt blue (0129), buttercup (0295) and gorse yellow (0304) small amount of each.

Fitting

Same for all.

1 button (for padding), 3 cm (1 1/16″) diameter.

1 brooch pin, bits of cotton.

Top···Soft pink cotton lace, 1.5 cm (5/8″) width, 18 cm (7″) length.

Bottom···Light blue cotton lace, 1.5 cm (5/8″) width, 18 cm (7″) length.

Left···White cotton lace, 1.5 cm (5/8″) width, 10 cm (3 7/8″) length.

Finished size

Top, bottom brooches···5 cm (2″) diameter.

Left brooch···3 cm (1 1/16″) diameter.

Directions

Copy patterns and embroider; assemble as shown.

How to make top and bottom brooches.

1. 0.4 cm
Cotton

Run gathering stitches around embroidery and place over button; stuff cotton in excess space and pull thread to make several stitches to cover opening.

2. Slip stitch

Ruffle lace with gathering stitches; slip stitch into place.

3.

Sew on felt circle, 2.5 cm in diameter (pink for top button, light blue for bottom); attach brooch pin.

How to make left brooch

Lace — Button
Felt — Side view — Sew on balls of lace all around

Follow step 1 for top/bottom brooches; sew on lace as shown; attach light blue felt circle, 2.5 cm in diameter, and brooch pin.

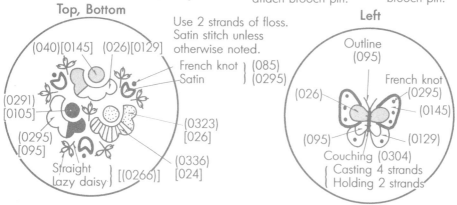

Top, Bottom

Use 2 strands of floss. Satin stitch unless otherwise noted.

(040)[0145] (026)[0129]

French knot } (085)
Satin } (0295)

(0291)[0105]

(0295)[095]

(0323)[026]

(0336)[024]

Straight
Lazy daisy } [(0266)]

Left

Outline (095)

French knot (0295)

(026)

(0145)

(095)

(0129)

Couching (0304)
{ Casting 4 strands
Holding 2 strands

75

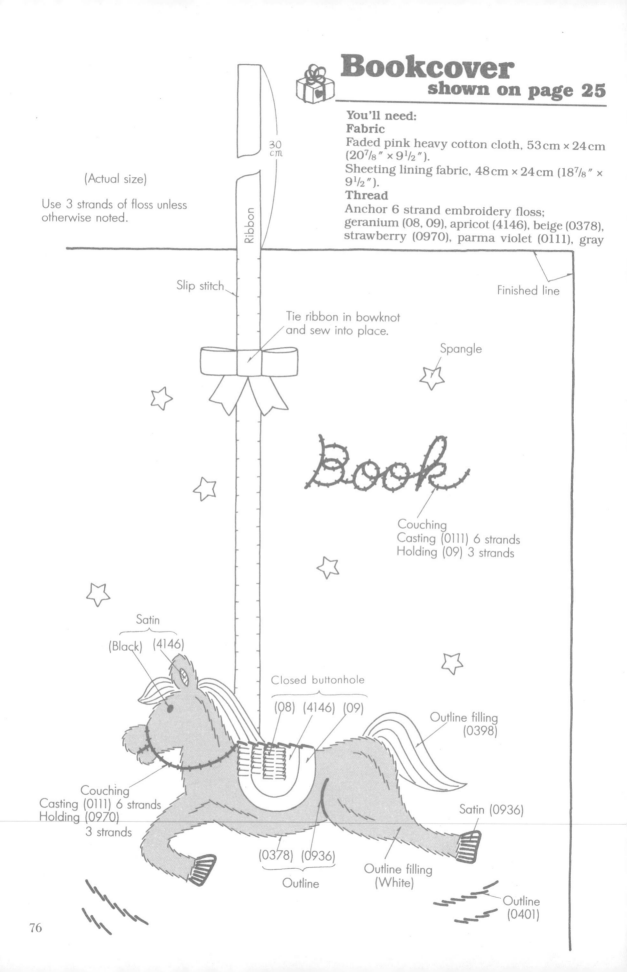

Bookcover
shown on page 25

You'll need:
Fabric
Faded pink heavy cotton cloth, 53 cm × 24 cm (20⅞″ × 9½″).
Sheeting lining fabric, 48 cm × 24 cm (18⅞″ × 9½″).
Thread
Anchor 6 strand embroidery floss; geranium (08, 09), apricot (4146), beige (0378), strawberry (0970), parma violet (0111), gray

(Actual size)

Use 3 strands of floss unless otherwise noted.

30 cm

Ribbon

Slip stitch

Tie ribbon in bowknot and sew into place.

Finished line

Spangle

Couching
Casting (0111) 6 strands
Holding (09) 3 strands

Satin

(Black) (4146)

Closed buttonhole

(08) (4146) (09)

Outline filling
(0398)

Couching
Casting (0111) 6 strands
Holding (0970)
3 strands

Satin (0936)

(0378) (0936)

Outline

Outline filling
(White)

Outline
(0401)

(0398, 0401), chocolate (0936), black and white small amount of each.

Fitting
White grosgrain, 0.7 cm width ($^1/_4$"), 60 cm (23"$^5/_8$") length. 6 gold star-shaped spangles.

Finished size
22 cm × 17 cm (8$^5/_8$" × 6$^3/_4$").

Directions
Copy pattern onto fabric and embroider;sew on tape to finished embroidery and assemble as shown.

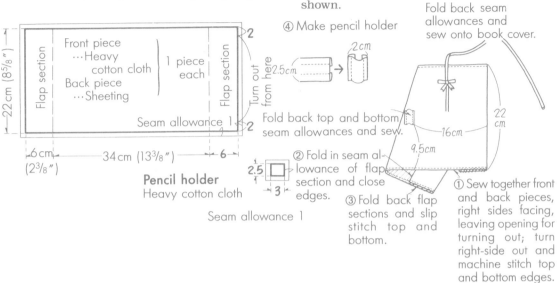

④ Make pencil holder

Fold back top and bottom seam allowances and sew.

② Fold in seam allowance of flap section and close edges.

③ Fold back flap sections and slip stitch top and bottom.

Fold back seam allowances and sew onto book cover.

① Sew together front and back pieces, right sides facing, leaving opening for turning out; turn right-side out and machine stitch top and bottom edges.

Pencil holder
Heavy cotton cloth

Seam allowance 1

Vanity Case shown on pages 28–29

C

You'll need:

Fabric

Zweigart Art 3609 BELFAST, forget-me-not blue, 81 cm × 14 cm (31$^7/_8$″ × 5$^1/_2$″). Cotton lining fabric, 81 cm × 15 cm (31$^7/_8$″ × 5$^7/_8$″).

Thread

Anchor 6 strand embroidery floss; jade (0188, 0186), amber gold (0309), golden tan (0363), cornflower (0145), cobalt blue (0130), carnation (026, 025), cardinal (040), lilac (0104), canary yellow (0289), haze (0920, 0922), dusky pink (0892), orange (0323) and white small amount of each.

Fitting

Zipper, 21 cm (8$^1/_8$″). 2 sets of small snap buttons. Padding, 81 cm × 14 cm (31$^7/_8$″ × 5$^1/_2$″).

Finished size

18.5 cm (7$^1/_4$″) width, 12.5 cm (4$^7/_8$″) depth.

Directions

Match centers of pattern and front outer piece; copy pattern and embroider; assemble as shown.

Add 0.5 cm seam allowance

Mouth section   Hemp 2 pieces

Tab section   Hemp 4 pieces

0.7   18.5   2.5   2.5   0.5

Front, Back
Outer piece
···Hemp
Inner piece
···Cotton cloth
Padding

2 pieces each

13.2 = Inner pie
12.5 = Padding
Outer pi

3   1.5
3

Gusset

Outer piece···Hemp, Inner piece···Cotton cloth, Padd
1 piece ea

2.5   Quilting   41   4   0.5

Assembly

⑤ ②
④   ① Snap button
③

Layer outer width piece and padding; quilt.

Follow steps ⑥-⑨ for Vanity Case D, p. 103, for directions ②-⑤

(Actual size)
Place flowers symmetrically.

A = (040)
B = (0289)
C = (0323)
D = (0104)

For each, French knot with 4 strands for ● 3 strands for ○ and 2 strands for •

Chain (0920) 4 strands
Embroider arches before flowers

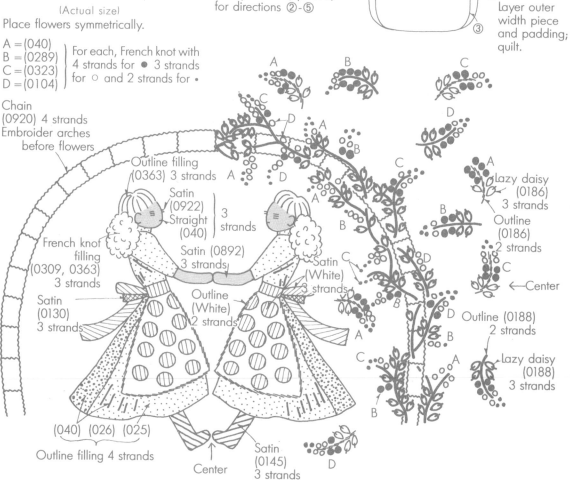

French knot filling (0309, 0363) 3 strands

Satin (0130) 3 strands

Outline filling (0363) 3 strands

Satin (0922) Straight (040)   3 strands

Satin (0892) 3 strands

Satin (White) 3 strands

Outline (White) 2 strands

(040) (026) (025)
Outline filling 4 strands

Center

Satin (0145) 3 strands

Lazy daisy (0186) 3 strands

Outline (0186) 2 strands

←Center

Outline (0188) 2 strands

Lazy daisy (0188) 3 strands

D

You'll need:

Fabric

Soft pink light silk, 80 cm × 20 cm (31$^1/_2$″ × 7$^7/_8$″).

Rayon lining fabric, 47 cm × 21 cm (18$^1/_2$″ × 8$^1/_4$″).

Thread

Anchor 6 strand embroidery floss; carnation (029, 028, 027, 026, 024), winter green (0878, 0877, 0876), violet (095), lilac (0105, 0104), peacock blue (0169, 0167), buttercup (0292) and white small amount of each.

Fitting

White tatting lace, 1.3 cm ($^1/_2$″) width, 110 cm (43$^1/_4$″) length. Purchased flower appliqués, 4 each of pink and blue, 2 yellows. 2 sets of small snap buttons. Zipper, 23 cm (9″). Padding for quilting, 47 cm × 21 cm (18$^1/_2$″ × 8$^1/_4$″).

Finished size

21 cm (8$^1/_4$″) width, 15 cm (5$^7/_8$″).

Directions

Copy pattern onto appliqué and embroider; assemble as shown.

Front (Actual size)

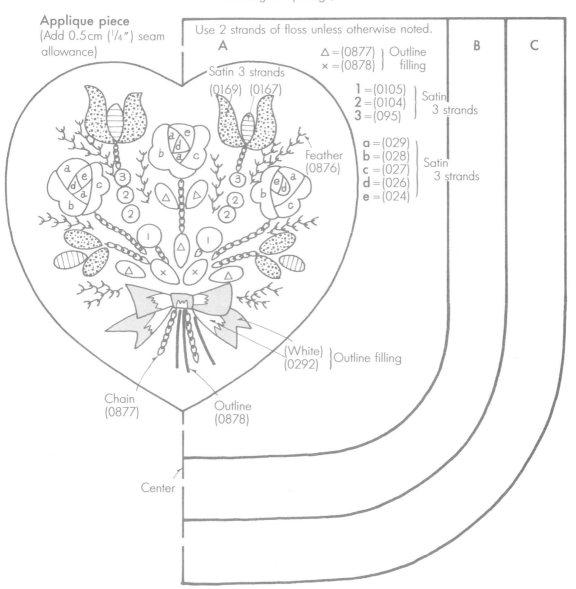

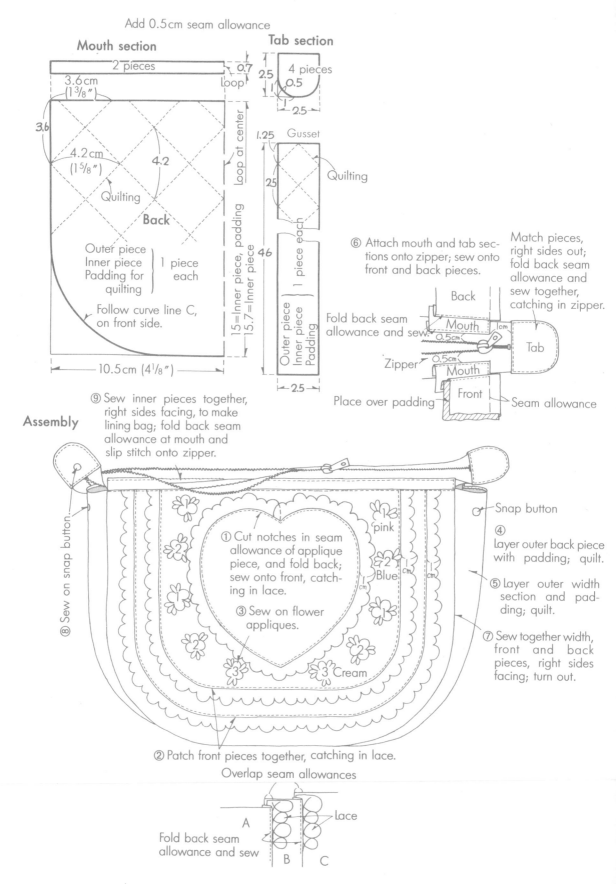

Add 0.5cm seam allowance

Mouth section

2 pieces

0.7 Loop

3.6cm (1 3/8")

3.6

4.2cm (1 5/8")   4.2

Quilting

Back

Outer piece
Inner piece
Padding for
quilting } 1 piece each

Follow curve line C, on front side.

10.5cm (4 1/8")

15=Inner piece, padding
15.7=Inner piece

Loop at center

Tab section

2.5   4 pieces   0.5

1

2.5

1.25   Gusset

2.5   Quilting

46

Outer piece
Inner piece
Padding } 1 piece each

2.5

⑥ Attach mouth and tab sections onto zipper; sew onto front and back pieces.

Match pieces, right sides out; fold back seam allowance and sew together, catching in zipper.

Back

Mouth   1cm

Fold back seam allowance and sew   0.5cm

Zipper   0.5cm

Mouth

Place over padding

Tab

Front

Seam allowance

Assembly

⑨ Sew inner pieces together, right sides facing, to make lining bag; fold back seam allowance at mouth and slip stitch onto zipper.

⑧ Sew on snap button

① Cut notches in seam allowance of applique piece, and fold back; sew onto front, catching in lace.

③ Sew on flower appliques.

1 pink

2 Blue

1 cm

3 Cream

2

3

Snap button

④ Layer outer back piece with padding; quilt.

⑤ Layer outer width section and padding; quilt.

⑦ Sew together width, front and back pieces, right sides facing; turn out.

② Patch front pieces together, catching in lace.

Overlap seam allowances

A

B   C

lace

Fold back seam allowance and sew

Miniature Frames (Right)
shown on page 37

Assembly

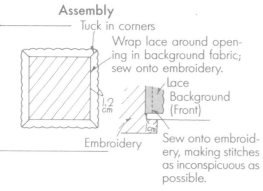

- Tuck in corners
- Wrap lace around opening in background fabric; sew onto embroidery.
- 1.2 cm
- Lace
- Background (Front)
- 1 cm
- Embroidery
- Sew onto embroidery, making stitches as inconspicuous as possible.

(Actual size)

You'll need:
Fabric
Zweigart Art 3711 ARIOSA, white 12cm (4³/₄″) square. White-on-green flower patterned fabric, 20cm (7⁷/₈″) square.

Thread
Anchor 6 strand embroidery floss; flesh pink (0883), carnation (026), geranium (09), terra-cotta (0336), parma violet (0108), cyclamen (085), peacock blue (0167) and jade (0188, 0185) small amount of each.

Fitting
Frame, 14cm (5¹/₂″) square in inner size.
White cotton lace 2cm (³/₄″) width.

Finished size
Same as frame size.

Directions
Embroider; cut fabric and assemble, following directions for top frame, page 51.

Outline filling (0883) 2 strands

Straight (0185) 2 strands

Outline (0336) 1 strand

Satin / Straight (0883) 2 strands

Satin (085) 2 strands

Straight (0167) 1 strand

←Center

Outline (0883) { 2 strands / 1 strand }

Outline (0167) 1 strand

Satin (09) 2 strands

Eyes, brows···Straight (0883) 1 strand
Mouth, cheeks···Straight (09) 1 strand

Couched trellis (0883) 1 strand

Outline filling (0108) 2 strands

Straight (0188) 2 strands   Lazy daisy

Outline (0108) 2 strands

Satin (0883) 2 strands   ↑ Center

Straight

Satin (026) 2 strands

 # Doily
shown on page 36

You'll need:
Fabric
Zweigart Art 1008 SULTA (87 stitches per 10cm), royal blue, 44cm × 22cm (17³/₈″ × 8⁵/₈″).

Thread
Anchor 6 strand embroidery floss; laurel green (0208), jade (0186), amber gold (0306), buttercup (0295), snuff brown (0374), peacock blue (0169, 0168), cornflower (0145), violet (095), cyclamen (085), dusky pink (0892), terra-cotta (0336) and gray (0400) small amount of each.

Fitting
Royal blue bias tape, 1.2cm (¹/₂″) width, 70cm (27¹/₂″) length.
White nylon lace, 2.5cm (1″) width, 150cm (59″) length.

Finished size
Refer to chart.

Directions
Copy pattern onto front piece and embroider; assemble as shown.

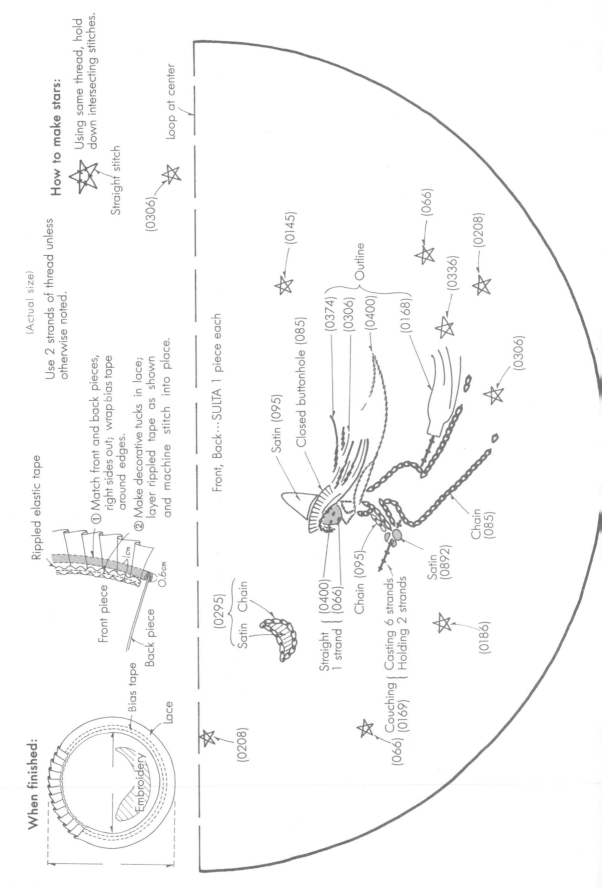

When finished:

Embroidery · Lace · Bias tape · Front piece · Back piece

Rippled elastic tape

1cm · 0.6cm

(Actual size)

Use 2 strands of thread unless otherwise noted.

How to make stars:

Using same thread, hold down intersecting stitches.

Straight stitch

(0306) Loop at center

① Match front and back pieces, right sides out; wrap bias tape around edges.

② Make decorative tucks in lace; layer rippled tape as shown and machine stitch into place.

Front, Back···SULTA 1 piece each

(0208) · (0145) · (066) · (0336) · (0208) · (0306) · (0186) · (066)

Satin (095)
Closed buttonhole (085)
(0374)
(0306)
(0400) Outline
(0168)
Chain (085)
Chain (095)
Satin (0892)
Straight { (0400) (066) } 1 strand
Couching { Casting 6 strands · Holding 2 strands } (066) (0169)
(0295) Satin Chain

Handkerchieves (A, B) shown on pages 28-29

You'll need:
Fabric
White handkerchief, 42cm (16$\frac{1}{2}$") square.
Thread
Anchor 6 strand embroidery floss;
A···carnation (028, 027), lilac (0104), winter green (0877, 0876), peacock blue (0169, 0167) and turquoise (0928) small amount of each.
B···winter green (0898, 0877, 0876), carnation (028, 024, 029, 026, 027), peacock blue (0169, 0167), buttercup (0292), violet (095) and white small amount of each.
Directions
A···Copy pattern onto corner of handkerchief and embroider.
B···Copy pattern for Vanity Case D, page 79, onto center of handkerchief; embroider.

A (Actual size)

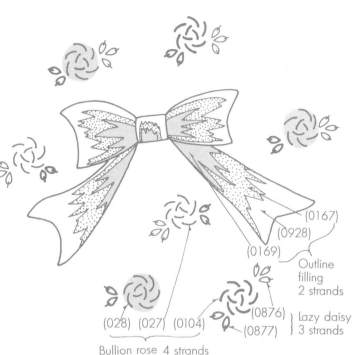

(0167)
(0928)
(0169)
Outline filling 2 strands

(028) (027) (0104)

(0876)
(0877)
Lazy daisy 3 strands

Bullion rose 4 strands

 # Miniature Cushion shown on page 45

You'll need:
Fabric
Top cushion···Light yellow broadcloth, cotton and lining fabric, 74cm × 37cm (29$\frac{1}{8}$" × 14$\frac{5}{8}$") each. Light yellow hemp, 21cm × 15cm (8$\frac{1}{4}$" × 5$\frac{7}{8}$").
Bottom cushion···Ash gray broadcloth, cotton lining fabric, 74cm × 37cm (29$\frac{1}{8}$" × 14$\frac{5}{8}$") each. Ash gray hemp, 21cm × 15cm (8$\frac{1}{4}$" × 5$\frac{7}{8}$").
Thread
DMC 6 strand embroidery floss;
Top···emerald green (955) geranium pink (894)

peony rose (957) geranium red (353) umber (435) tangerine yellow (744) parma violet (210) azure blue (3325) small amount of each.
Bottom···same as for top cushion.
Fitting (for one cushion)
Padding for quilting, 74cm × 37cm (29$\frac{1}{8}$" × 14$\frac{5}{8}$").
White cotton lace, 2cm ($\frac{3}{4}$") width, 100cm (39$\frac{3}{8}$") length.
Inner cushion stuffed with 200 grams of fiberfill.

Asembly

② Fold back seam allowance on applique; machine stitch onto center of front piece, catching in ruffled lace.

Front, back

2 (1 cm all around)

Quilting

35cm (13$\frac{3}{4}$")

35 3.5

2

Outer piece
···Broadcloth
Inner piece
···Cotton cloth
Padding for quilting

2 pieces each

1.5

9

9 1.5

35cm (13$\frac{3}{4}$")

Figures insides parenthesis indicate seam allowance.

Applique
(1 cm all around)

13cm (5$\frac{1}{8}$")

Hemp

19cm (7$\frac{1}{2}$") ④

Turn out and stuff with filled inner cushion; slip stitch opening.

Turn out from here

① Layer outer, padding, and inner pieces for both front and back sides; quilt, making 3.5cm squares.

③ Sew pieces together, right sides facing, leaving opening for turning out.

83

Finished size
35 cm (13³/₄″) square.

Directions
Match centers of appliqué fabric and pattern; copy pattern and embroider. Assemble as shown.

Use design as shown for flower basket. Use 4 strands of floss and closed buttonhole stitch unless otherwise noted.

Numbers inside parenthesis for top; those in brackets for bottom.

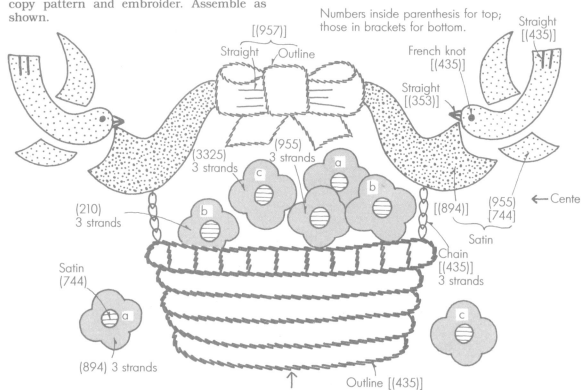

Substitute hearts for flowers for lower cushion (satin stitch).

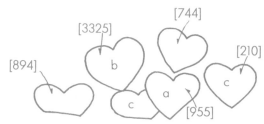

Embroider heart (a) to left of basket, heart (c) to the right.

 # Cape (F)   shown on pages 32–33

You'll need:
Fabric
Zweigart Art 3609 BELFAST, white 80 cm × 45 cm (31¹/₂″ × 17³/₄″).
Thread
Anchor 6 strand embroidery floss; carnation (026, 025), cobalt blue (0130), violet (095) and moss green (0265) 0.5 skein each, canary yellow (0291) small amount.

Fitting
Magenta rose ribbon, 0.8 cm (³/₈″) width, 370 cm (145⁵/₈″) length.
White cotton lace, 5 cm (2″) width, 200 cm (78³/₈″) length (see picture).
Finished size
Refer to chart.
Directions
Copy patterns symmetrically as shown; embroider and assemble as directed.

(Actual size)   Use 2 strands of floss unless otherwise noted.

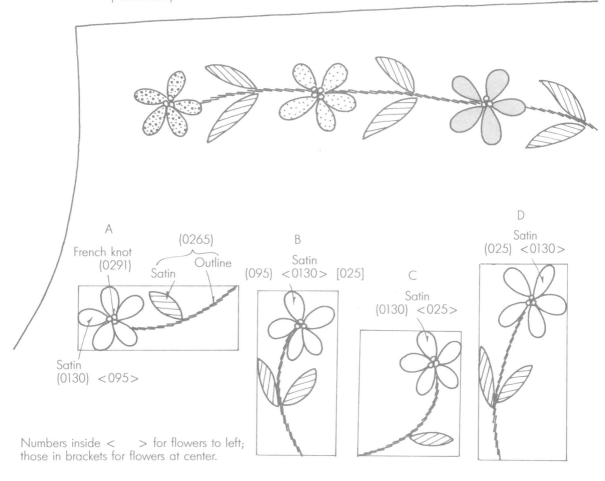

A

French knot
(0291)

(0265)

Satin   Outline

Satin
(0130) <095>

B

Satin
(095) <0130> [025]

C

Satin
(0130) <025>

D

Satin
(025) <0130>

Numbers inside <   > for flowers to left;
those in brackets for flowers at center.

Add 1 cm seam allowance all around,
except for neckline.
Designs should be placed symmetrically.

Assembly

③ Machine stitch ribbon
onto neckline.

① Sew lace onto
cape, right sides
facing.

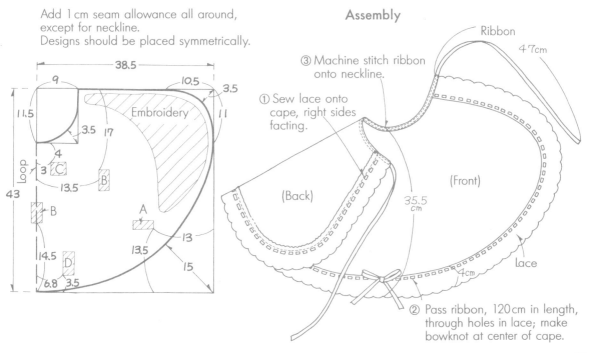

② Pass ribbon, 120 cm in length,
through holes in lace; make
bowknot at center of cape.

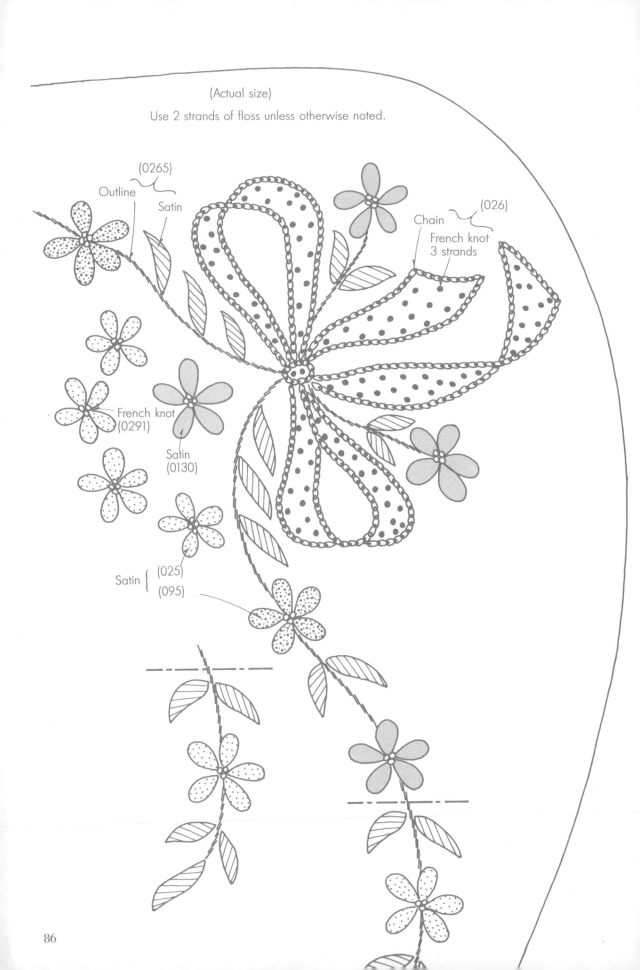

(Actual size)

Use 2 strands of floss unless otherwise noted.

(0265)

Outline

Satin

Chain

(026)

French knot
3 strands

French knot
(0291)

Satin
(0130)

Satin { (025)
         (095)

Jar Covers (H, I)

You'll need:
Fabric
Broadcloth, 25 cm × 19 cm (9⁷/₈″ × 7¹/₂″), white for H, canary yellow for I.
Thread
DMC 6 strand embroidery floss;
H···moss green (472), cerise (604, 602), raspberry red (3689, 3687) and plum (553) small amount of each.
I···parakeet green (907), tangerine yellow (742), saffron (727, 725), lemon yellow (307) and moss green (472) small amount of each.
Fitting
Cotton lace, 2.5 cm (1″) width, 33 cm (13″) length, white for H, canary yellow for I.
Bias tape, 1.2 cm (¹/₂″) width, 120 cm (47¹/₄″) length, white for H, canary yellow for I.
Adhesive padding, 5 cm (2″) square each.
Finished size
Refer to chart.
Directions
Copy pattern onto fabric and embroider; assemble as shown, and tie ribbon around elastic section.

(Actual size)

Use 2 strands of floss.

Numbers inside parenthesis for H; those in brackets for I.

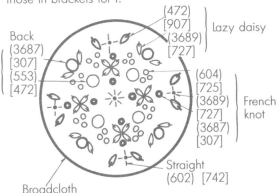

(472) [907] (3689) [727] Lazy daisy

Back (3687) [307] (553) [472]

(604) (725) (3689) (727) (3687) [307] French knot

Straight (602) [742]

Broadcloth (Add 0.5 cm seam allowance) Adhesive backing (Cut to size)

① Trim with bias tape. 0.6 cm

Background Broadcloth Lace Embroidery Pass elastic here 0.8 3 19 cm (7¹/₂″) (Cut to size)

④ Make passage for elastic (Wrong side). Elastic Place bias tape on wrong side and machine stitch both ends; pass elastic through opening.

Adhesive padding ② Place adhesive backbacking behind embroidery; sew around seam allowance and pull thread to fit.

Background, front Embroidery, front Lace 2 cm Adhesive padding 0.5 cm

③ Place ruffled lace between background fabric and embroidery; machine stitch layers together.

 # Coasters

D, E
You'll need:
Fabric
Broadcloth, 9 cm (3¹/₂″) square each, white and blue for D, white and pink for E.
Thread
DMC 6 strand embroidery floss;
D···sevres blue (799), forget-me-not blue (813), royal blue (797) and lemon yellow (307) small amount of each.
E···peony rose (957), lemon yellow (307), garnet red (335), soft pink (766) small amount of each.

Fitting
Purchased frills, 2 cm (³/₄″) width, 30 cm (11³/₄″) length, polka-dotted, blue for D, pink for E.
Adhesive padding, 16 cm × 8 cm (6¹/₄″ × 3¹/₈″) each.
Finished size
11 cm (4³/₈″) square.
Directions
Copy pattern onto fabric and embroider; assemble as shown.

(Actual size) Use 2 strands of floss.
Back stitch unless otherwise noted.

Numbers inside parenthesis for D; those in brackets for E.

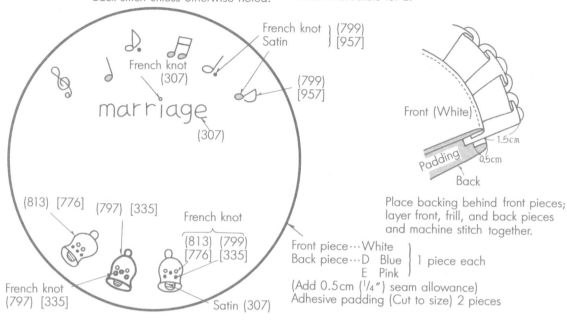

French knot } (799)
Satin } [957]

French knot
(307)

(799)
[957]

marriage
(307)

(813) [776]   (797) [335]

French knot

(813) (799)
[776] [335]

French knot
(797) [335]

Satin (307)

Front (White)

1.5cm

Padding   0.5cm

Back

Place backing behind front pieces;
layer front, frill, and back pieces
and machine stitch together.

Front piece···White
Back piece···D Blue } 1 piece each
          E Pink
(Add 0.5cm (¹/₄″) seam allowance)
Adhesive padding (Cut to size) 2 pieces

F, G
You'll need:
Fabric (for one coaster)
Powder green broadcloth, 21 cm × 11 cm
(8¹/₄″ × 4³/₈″).

Thread
DMC 6 strand embroidery floss;
F···soft pink (776, 818), peony rose (957),
brilliant green (704) small amount of each.
G···lemon yellow (307), tangerine yellow (743),
saffron (727) and brilliant green (704) small
amount of each.

Fitting
(for one)
Adhesive padding, 11 cm
(4³/₈″) square. light
green bias tape, 1.2 cm
(¹/₂″) width, 35 cm (13³/₄″)
length.
Directions
Copy pattern onto outer
piece and embroider; place
adhesive backing between
outer and inner pieces;
trim edges with bias tape.

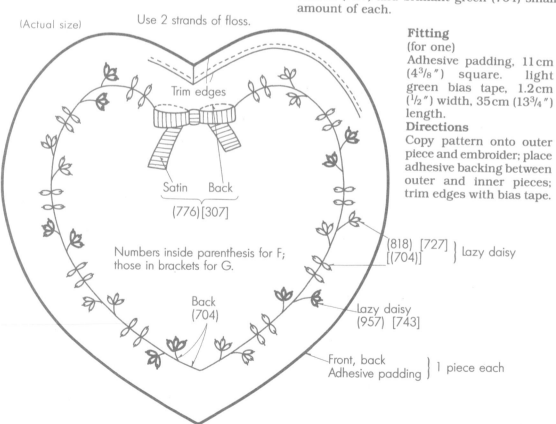

(Actual size)   Use 2 strands of floss.

Trim edges

Satin   Back

(776)[307]

Numbers inside parenthesis for F;
those in brackets for G.

Back
(704)

(818) [727]
[(704)] } lazy daisy

Lazy daisy
(957) [743]

Front, back
Adhesive padding } 1 piece each

🎀 Apron shown on page 53

(Actual size)

Use 3 strands of floss.
Outline stitch unless otherwise noted.

(08) (073)
Satin

(White)

(0398)

Satin
(4146) (09)

(09)

(4146)

(073)

(09)

(08)

You'll need:

Fabric
White broadcloth, 86 cm × 100 cm (33⅞" × 39⅜").

Thread
Anchor 6 strand embroidery floss; geranium (09, 08), apricot (4146), old rose (073), gray (0398) and white small amount of each.

Fitting
White cotton lace, 2 cm (¾") width, 260 cm (102⅜") length.

Finished size
Refer to chart.

Directions
Copy patterns onto apron according to picture; embroider and assemble as shown.

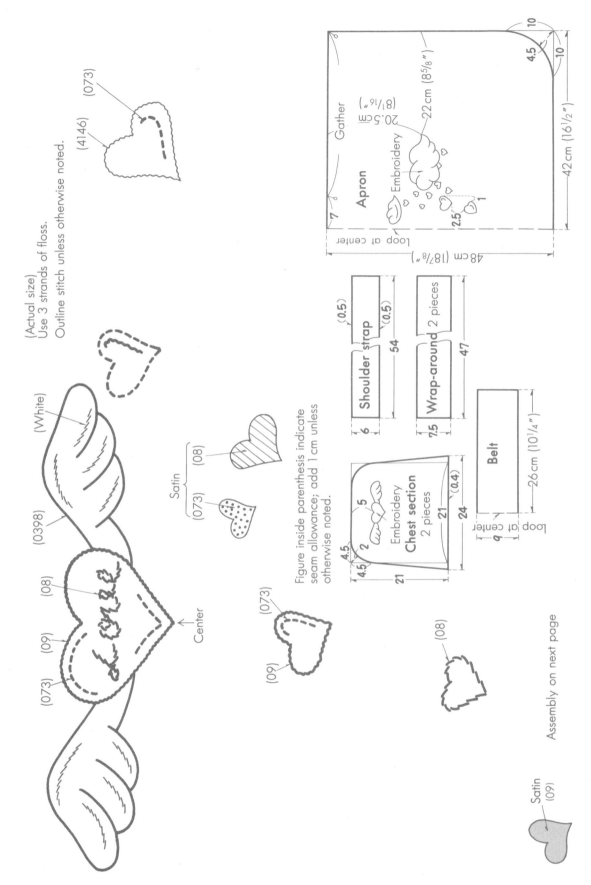

(Actual size)
Use 3 strands of floss.
Outline stitch unless otherwise noted.

(4146)   (073)

(White)

(0398)

(08)

(09)

(073)   ← Center

Satin { (08)   (073)

Figure inside parenthesis indicate
seam allowance; add 1 cm unless
otherwise noted.

(073)

(09)

Apron   Gather

Embroidery   22 cm (8⅝")   20.5 cm (8¹/₁₆")

1

2.5

7

Loop at center

48 cm (18⅞")

4.5   10   10

42 cm (16½")

(0.5)   Shoulder strap   (0.5)   54   6

(0.5)   Wrap-around 2 pieces   47   7.5

Embroidery
Chest section
2 pieces

5   (0.4)

4.5   2   21   24

4.5   21

Belt   26 cm (10¼")

Loop at center   9

(08)

Assembly on next page

Satin
(09)

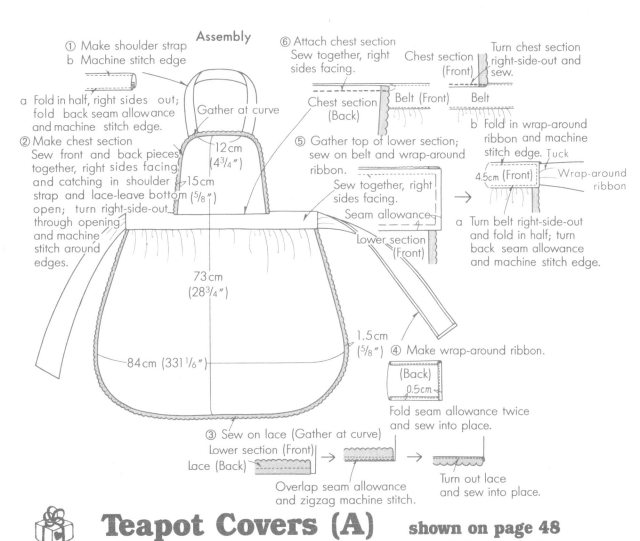

Assembly

① Make shoulder strap
b Machine stitch edge

a Fold in half, right sides out; fold back seam allowance and machine stitch edge.

② Make chest section
Sew front and back pieces together, right sides facing, and catching in shoulder strap and lace-leave bottom open; turn right-side-out through opening and machine stitch around edges.

Gather at curve

12 cm (4³⁄₄")

15 cm (5⁄₈")

73 cm (28³⁄₄")

84 cm (33 1⁄₆")

1.5 cm (5⁄₈")

③ Sew on lace (Gather at curve)
Lower section (Front)
Lace (Back)

Overlap seam allowance and zigzag machine stitch.

Turn out lace and sew into place.

⑥ Attach chest section
Sew together, right sides facing.

Chest section (Back)

Chest section (Front)

Belt (Front)

⑤ Gather top of lower section; sew on belt and wrap-around ribbon.
Sew together, right sides facing.
Seam allowance

Lower section (Front)

④ Make wrap-around ribbon.

(Back)
0.5 cm

Fold seam allowance twice and sew into place.

Turn chest section right-side-out and sew.

Belt

b Fold in wrap-around ribbon and machine stitch edge. Tuck

4.5 cm (Front)

Wrap-around ribbon

a Turn belt right-side-out and fold in half; turn back seam allowance and machine stitch edge.

Teapot Covers (A) shown on page 48

You'll need:

Fabric

Parma violet, white terrycloth, 40 cm × 31 cm (15³⁄₄" × 12¹⁄₄") each.
Flannel, 80 cm × 31 cm (31¹⁄₂" × 12¹⁄₄").
Pink broadcloth, 30 cm (11³⁄₄") square.

Thread

DMC 6 strand embroidery floss;
parakeet green (907, 906), moss green (469), peony rose (957), soft pink (776), cerise (603), lemon yellow (307), parma violet (209), indian red (3041) and chestnut (407) small amount of each.

Finished size

Refer to chart.

Directions

Cut out fabric; copy pattern onto one white outer piece and embroider; assemble as shown.

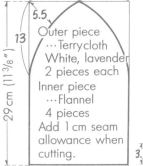

5.5

13

Outer piece
···Terrycloth
White, lavender
2 pieces each
Inner piece
···Flannel
4 pieces
Add 1 cm seam allowance when cutting.

29 cm (11³⁄₈")

18 cm (7¹⁄₁₆")

② Sew inner pieces together, right sides facing; make cleavage in seam allowance.

Trimming fabric

3.5

Braodcloth

74 (Path together)

Assembly

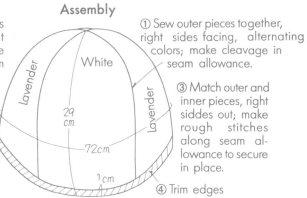

Lavender

White

Lavender

29 cm

72 cm

1 cm

① Sew outer pieces together, right sides facing, alternating colors; make cleavage in seam allowance.

③ Match outer and inner pieces, right siddes out; make rough stitches along seam allowance to secure in place.

④ Trim edges

91

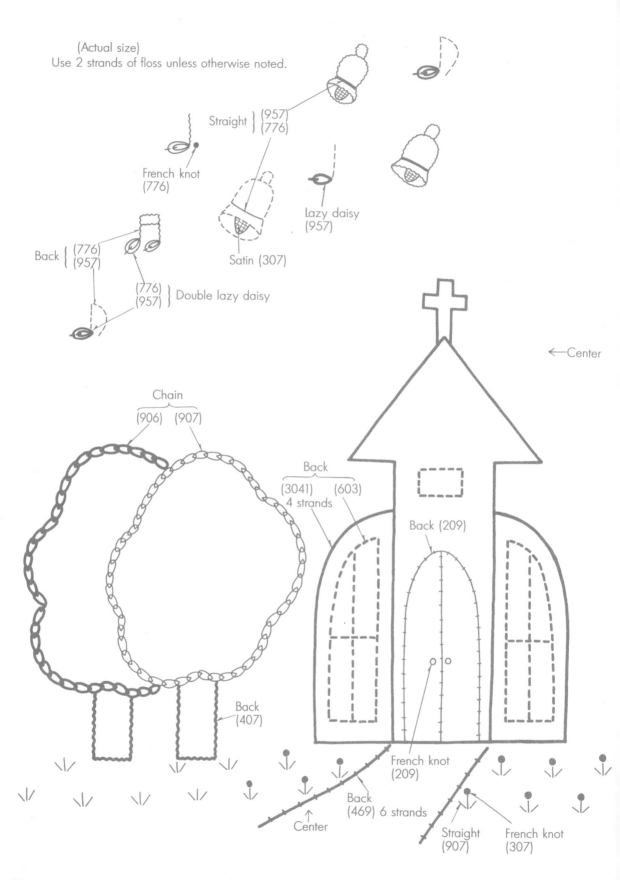

(Actual size)
Use 2 strands of floss unless otherwise noted.

Straight } (957)
(776)

French knot
(776)

Lazy daisy
(957)

Back { (776)
(957)

Satin (307)

(776)
(957) } Double lazy daisy

←Center

Chain
(906) (907)

Back
(3041) (603)
4 strands

Back (209)

Back
(407)

French knot
(209)

Back
(469) 6 strands

↑
Center

Straight
(907)

French knot
(307)

92

Wall Hangings shown on page 40

You'll need:
Fabric
Zweigart Art 3609 BELFAST, Top⋯sevres blue, 30cm × 16cm (11³/₄″ × 6¹/₄″), white, 14cm (5¹/₂″) square; Bottom⋯cornflower blue, 30cm × 16cm (11³/₄″ × 6¹/₄″), white, 14cm (5¹/₂″) square.
Thread
Anchor 6 strand embroidery floss;
Top⋯turquoise (0928), peacock blue (0168), navy blue (0150), linen (0392, 0390), sea blue (0976), parma violet (0108) and scarlet (047) small amount of each.
Bottom⋯lilac (0105), mauve (0869), almond green (0263), coffee (0905), linen (0391, 0390), geranium (09), scarlet (047), apricot (4146) and ecru (0926) small amount of each.

Fitting
11 pearl-colored round beads (small) for each. Adhesive padding 15cm (5⁷/₈″) square each. Ribbon, 0.6cm (¹/₄″) width, 40cm (15³/₈″) length, sevres blue for top, parma violet for bottom.
Finished size
Refer to chart.
Directions
Copy pattern onto applique fabric and embroider; assemble as shown.

Add 0.5cm seam allowance for front, back, and applique pieces.
Cut adhesive padding to size.

② Place adhesive backing on back piece; match front and back pieces, right sides out; fold in seam allowance and sew pieces together.

① Fold back seam allowance and applique onto front piece.

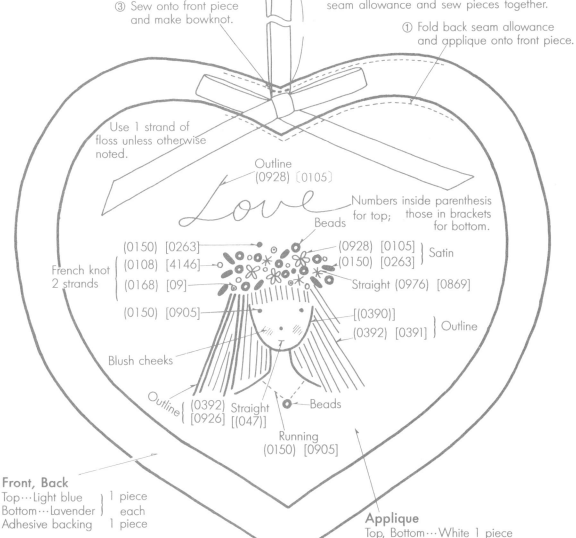

③ Sew onto front piece and make bowknot.

Use 1 strand of floss unless otherwise noted.

Outline (0928) [0105]

Beads

Numbers inside parenthesis for top; those in brackets for bottom.

(0150) [0263]
(0108) [4146]
(0168) [09]

French knot 2 strands

(0928) [0105]
(0150) [0263] } Satin

Straight (0976) [0869]

(0150) [0905]

[(0390)]
(0392) [0391] } Outline

Blush cheeks

Outline { (0392) [0926] Straight [(047)]

Beads

Running (0150) [0905]

Front, Back
Top⋯Light blue } 1 piece
Bottom⋯Lavender } each
Adhesive backing   1 piece

Applique
Top, Bottom⋯White 1 piece

Coasters (C, D, E) shown on page 57

You'll need:
Fabric
Sheeting C···Pink 18cm × 16cm (7$^1/_{16}$″ × 6$^1/_4$″), rose pink 12cm × 8cm (4$^3/_4$″ × 3$^1/_8$″).
D···Sky blue 18cm × 16cm (7$^1/_{16}$″ × 6$^1/_4$″), ash gray 12cm × 8cm (4$^3/_4$″ × 3$^1/_8$″).
E···Pink 14cm (5$^1/_2$″) square, white 12cm × 8cm (4$^3/_4$″ × 3$^1/_8$″), ash gray 8cm (3$^1/_8$″) square.
Thread
DMC 6 strand embroidery floss;
C···green (3053), peacock blue (807), beige (3024), smoke gray (640), cream (746), lemon yellow (445), parma violet (209) and old rose (3354) small amount of each.
D···pistachio green (367), lemon yellow (445), sky blue (747), indigo (823), ash gray (762), peacock blue (807) and old rose (3354) small amount of each.

E···peacock blue (807), sky blue (747), beaver gray (645), smoke gray (644), lemon yellow (445) and geranium red (353) small amount of each.
Fitting
Padding for quilting, 11cm (4$^3/_8$″) square each.
Finished size
Refer to chart.
Directions
Patch pieces together as shown; copy patterns and embroider. Match outer and inner pieces, right sides out, and place padding in between; wrap inner piece around edges of outer piece, as shown, and slip stitch into place. Quilt as shown.

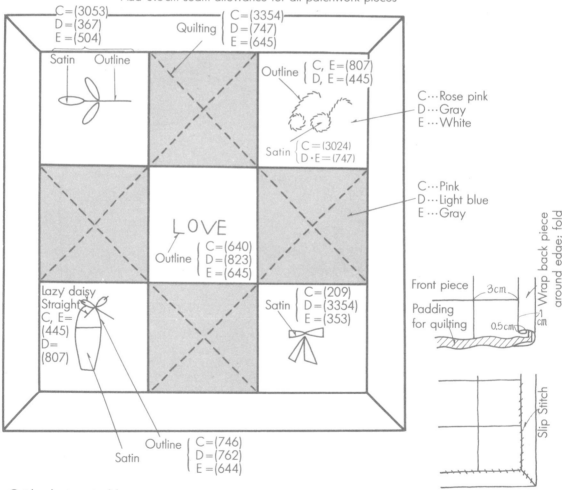

Cut back piece to 14cm square.
C, E···Pink D···Light blue
Cut padding for quilting to 11 cm square.

Doilies (F, G)
shown on page 57

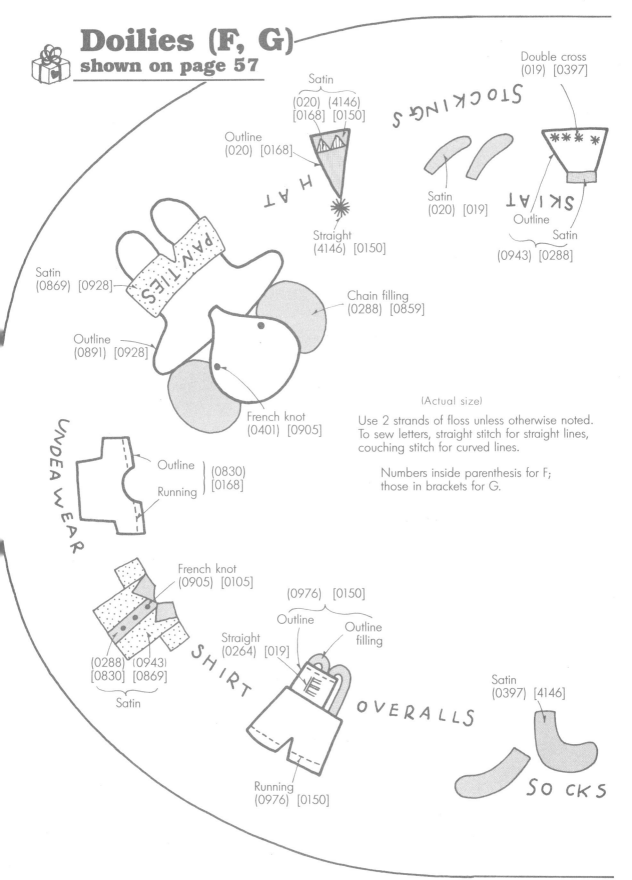

Double cross
(019) [0397]

Satin
(020) (4146)
[0168] [0150]

STOCKINGS

Outline
(020) [0168]

HAT

Satin
(020) [019]

SKIRT

Outline   Satin

(0943) [0288]

Straight
(4146) [0150]

PANTIES

Satin
(0869) [0928]

Chain filling
(0288) [0859]

Outline
(0891) [0928]

French knot
(0401) [0905]

(Actual size)

Use 2 strands of floss unless otherwise noted.
To sew letters, straight stitch for straight lines,
couching stitch for curved lines.

Numbers inside parenthesis for F;
those in brackets for G.

UNDEAWEAR

Outline } (0830)
Running } [0168]

French knot
(0905) [0105]

(0976) [0150]

Outline

Outline
filling

Straight
(0264) [019]

(0288) (0943)
[0830] [0869]

Satin

SHIRT

OVERALLS

Satin
(0397) [4146]

Running
(0976) [0150]

SOCKS

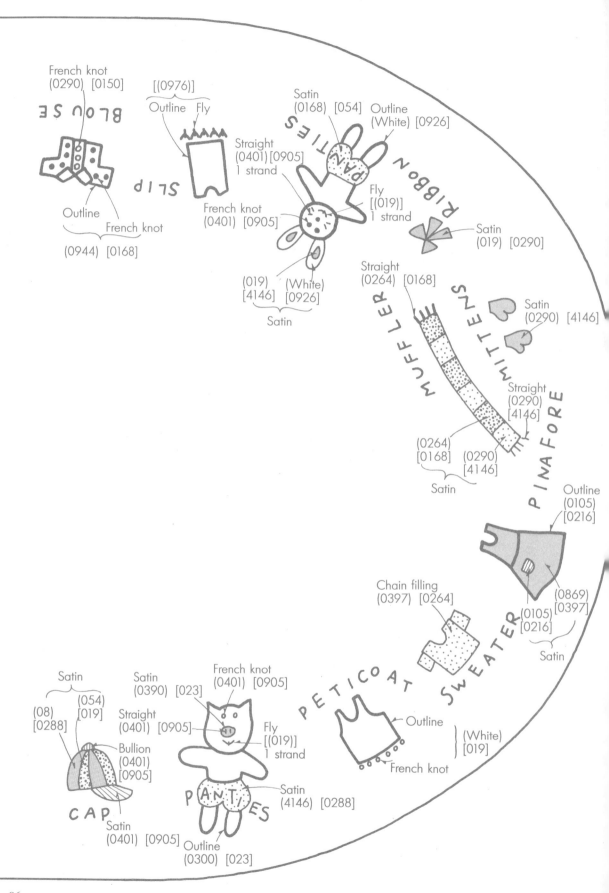

BLOUSE

French knot
(0290) [0150]

Outline
French knot
(0944) [0168]

SLIP

[(0976)]
Outline   Fly

Straight
(0401) [0905]
1 strand

French knot
(0401) [0905]

(019)   (White)
[4146]   [0926]

Satin

PANTIES

Satin
(0168) [054]   Outline
(White) [0926]

Fly
[(019)]
1 strand

RIBBON

Satin
(019) [0290]

MUFFLER

Straight
(0264) [0168]

(0264)
[0168]   (0290)
[4146]

Satin

MITTENS

Satin
(0290) [4146]

Straight
(0290)
[4146]

PINAFORE

Outline
(0105)
[0216]

(0869)
(0105) [0397]
[0216]

Satin

SWEATER

Chain filling
(0397) [0264]

PETICOAT

Outline

(White)
[019]

French knot

CAP

Satin

(08)   (054)
[0288]   [019]

Satin
(0390) [023]

Straight
(0401) [0905]

Bullion
(0401)
[0905]

Satin
(0401) [0905]

French knot
(0401) [0905]

Fly
[(019)]
1 strand

PANTIES

Satin
(4146) [0288]

Outline
(0300) [023]

You'll need:

Fabric
Broadcloth, 34 cm × 23 cm (13⅜″ × 9″), pink for F, white for G.

Thread
Anchor 6 strand embroidery floss;
F···maize (0943), linen (0391), stone (0830), lilac (0105), mauve (0869, 0944), apricot (4146), cardinal (020, 019), rose pink (054), canary yellow (0288, 0290), gorse yellow (0300), coffee (0905), gray (0401, 0397), sea blue (0976), peacock blue (0168), moss green (0264), forest green (0214), geranium (08) and white small amount of each.
G···forest green (0216), gray (0397), mist green (0859), lilac (0105), mauve (0869), canary yellow (0290, 0288), sea blue (0976), navy blue (0150), peacock blue (0168), turquoise (0928), cardinal (019), apricot (4146), rose pink (054), carnation (023), moss green (0264), écru (0926), stone (0830) and coffee (905) small amount of each.

Fitting
Bias tape of broadcloth, 2 cm (¾″) width, 100 cm (39⅜″) length, yellow for E, pink for G.

Finished size
Refer to chart.

Directions
Copy pattern onto fabric and embroider; trim edges to finish.

Assembly

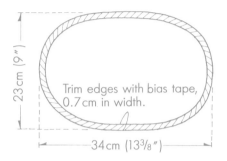

23 cm (9″)

Trim edges with bias tape, 0.7 cm in width.

34 cm (13⅜″)

Miniature Cushions   shown on page 61

Top, Middle

You'll need:

Fabric (for one cushion)
Indigo velveteen, 79 cm × 38 cm (31⅛″ × 15″).
White linen, 19 cm (7½″) square.

Thread
Anchor 6 strand embroidery floss;
Top···grass green (0246) 0.5 skein, almond green (0263), moss green (0267, 0268), maize (0942, 0943), parrot green (0258), flame (0332, 0334), tangerine (0316), raspberry (068, 066), gorse yellow (0303, 0302), cardinal (042), geranium (011), chestnut (0351), cinnamon (0367), beige (0376), forest green (0216, 0215), cornflower (0144), apple green (0230), peat brown (0380) and white small amount of each.
Middle···grass green (0246) 0.5 skein, almond green (0263), moss green (0267, 0268),

kingfisher (0164), sea blue (0978), cornflower (0144, 0145), jade (0188), maize (0943, 0942), parrot green (0258), violet (0100), cinnamon (0367), peat brown (0380), forest green (0216, 0215), apple green (0230), delphinium (0121), navy blue (0149) and white small amount of each.

Fitting (for one cushion)
Piping tape, 220 cm (86⅝″) length, sky blue for top cushion, purple for middle.
Zipper, 27 cm (10⅝″).
Inner cushion, filled with 200 grams of fiberfill.

Finished size
35 cm (13¾″) square.

Directions
Copy pattern onto appliqué fabric and embroider; sew zipper onto back piece and assemble as shown; stuff with inner cushion.

① Applique onto center of front piece.

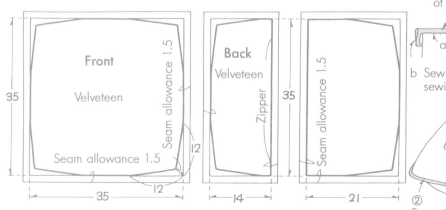

Piping tape

Assembly

a Fold back margin and slip stitch.

b Sew onto front piece, sewing inner recess.

Piping tape

② Sew pieces together, right sides facing and catching in tape; turn right-side-out.

Front — Velveteen — Seam allowance 1.5 — 35 — 12

Back — Velveteen — Zipper — 14

Seam allowance 1.5 — 35 — 21

(Actual size)
Use. 4 strands of floss unles
otherwise noted.
Numbers inside
parenthesis for
top; those in brackets
for middle.

Applique

Hemp   Add 1 cm folding
       margin when cutting.

Chain 3 strands

Outline
[[0558]] [[0246]] [[0230]] [[0216]]

long and short
[[White]]

Outline [[0144]]

Outline
[[0216]]

4 strands
1 strand   } Outline [[0216]]

Satin
[[0246]]
3 strands

Random stitch [[0216]]
1 strand

Outline filling

Chain
[[0268]]
3 strands

Chain
[[0258]]
3 strands

Satin
[[0216]]
3 strands

Random
stitch
[[0215]]
1 strand

Center→

Center→

Center Outline filling

[[0942]]
3 strands

[[0943]]
3 strands

[[0376]]
[[0367]]
3 strands

[[0263]]

[[0246]] [[0258]]
long and short, closed

Outline filling

Outline filling

[[0367]]
3 strands

[[0380]]
} Outline

[042]
[0164]

a = (0316) [0123]
b = (0332) [0978] } Closed
c = (0334) [0188] } buttonhole
d = (0316) [0978]
e = (0332) [0123]

1 = (042) [0149]   Chain filling
                    3 strands

2 = (0351) [0100]
3 = (0302) [0145]   } Outline
4 = (0303) [0121]   } filling
5 = (0351) [0188]
6 = (011) [0149]

Ⓐ = (042) [0162]
Ⓑ = (011) [0149] } Satin
Ⓒ = (0334) [0123]

○ = (042) [0164] } Closed
× = (066) [0168] } herringbone
△ = (068) [0162]

[[0267]] } long and short closed
[[0246]] } buttonhole 6 strands

Bottom
You'll need:
Fabric

Flower-on beige printed fabric, 79 cm × 38 cm (31 1/8″ × 15″). Pink linen, 15 cm (5 7/8″) square.

Thread

Anchor 6 strand embroidery floss; raspberry (068, 066), rose pink (054), cardinal (020), flame (0332, 0334), buttercup (0297), gorse yellow (0303), cornflower (0415), silver green (0945), maize (0944), peat brown (0380) and forest green (0215) small amount of each.

Fitting

White cotton lace, 3 cm (1 1/8″) width, 320 cm (126″) length.

Pink piping tape, 42 cm (16 1/2″) length. Zipper, 27 cm (10 5/8″).

Inner cushion with 200 grams of fiberfill.

Finished size

35 cm (13 3/4″) square.

Directions

Copy pattern onto appliqué fabric and embroider; sew zipper onto back piece and assemble as shown; stuff with inner cushion.

Assembly

Use printed fabric for front and back pieces; cut as for top and middle cushions.

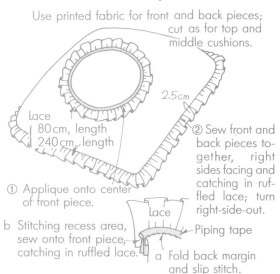

lace 80 cm, length
240 cm, length

2.5 cm

① Applique onto center of front piece.

b Stitching recess area, sew onto front piece, catching in ruffled lace.

② Sew front and back pieces together, right sides facing and catching in ruffled lace; turn right-side-out.

lace

Piping tape

a Fold back margin and slip stitch.

Use 3 strands of floss unless otherwise noted.

Tree trunk···Outline filling
(0380) 6 strands
Fill with outline stitches
(0994) 1 strand

Grass···Straight
— (0215) 1 strand
~ (0215) 3 strands
~ (0268) 6 strands
━ (0258) 6 strands
background

Applique (Actual size)
Hemp   Add 1 cm seam allowance when cutting.

French knot (0297)

Double lazy daisy (0268) 6 strands

Satin (066) (068)

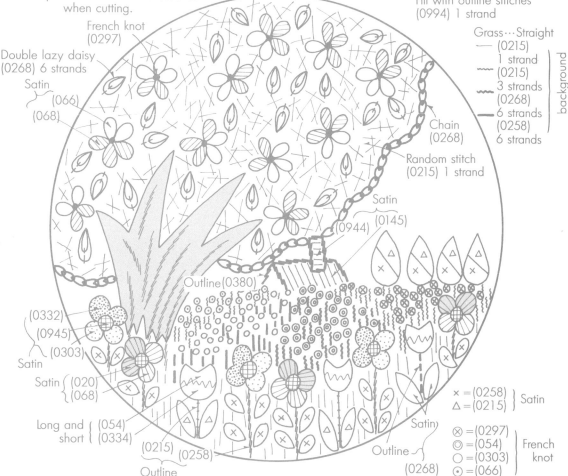

Chain (0268)

Random stitch (0215) 1 strand

Satin (0944) (0145)

Outline (0380)

(0332) (0945) (0303) Satin

Satin (020) (068)

Long and short (054) (0334)

(0215) (0258) Outline

Satin

Outline (0268)

x = (0258)
△ = (0215) } Satin

⊗ = (0297)
◎ = (054)
○ = (0303)
⊙ = (066) } French knot